The Lies of Becoming

Become a Better You, Build a Scalable Business

Tanya Kelker

The Writers Game

The Lies of Becoming

Become a Better You, Build a Scalable Business

Tanya Kelker

The Writers Game

"You are designed not to starve, sacrifice nor struggle. You are here to thrive, succeed and empower the world. When you realize YOU power, So will the world around you." - **Tanya Kelker**

Disclaimer

This book is for educational purposes only. The views expressed are those of the author alone. The reader is responsible for his or her own actions. Adherence to all applicable laws and regulations, including international, federal, state and local governing professional licensing, business practices, advertising and all other aspects of doing business in The United States, Canada or any other jurisdiction is the sole responsibility of the purchaser or reader. Neither the author nor the publisher assumes any responsibility or liability whatsoever on the behalf of the purchasers or reader of these materials.

THE LIES OF BECOMING

The Writers Game

8936 Northpointe Executive Park Drive, Ste 260,

Huntersville, NC 28078

info@thewritersgame.com

www.thewritersgame.com

ISBN: 979-8-9875189-4-6

eBook ISBN: 979-8-9875189-5-3

Printed in The United States of America

Contents

Dedication   VIII

Lies of Becoming   IX

1. WHO ARE YOU, REALLY?   1

2. DESIGNING THE LIFE YOU ENVISION   30

3. GOOD IDEAS VS. GOD IDEAS   51

4. WHAT IS POURED IN, FLOWS OUTWARD   72

5. MISSION MANIFESTATION IS POSSIBLE   83

6. PERMISSION GRANTED   102

7. BIRTHING THE CEO WITHIN   121

About Author   141

To the woman that's been stopped in her path, halted from her destiny and is experiencing hurdles in her journey; this book is your roadmap, guide and blueprint to becoming a better you so you can be prepared to succeed in the war of entrepreneurship.

To all that inspired, coached, challenged and empowered me in any way, I thank you for your tireless service, time and blessing. Without you, I wouldn't have the opportunity to empower others.

Lies of Becoming

"Envision the kind of woman you want to become and start to be her now." - Rachel Rodgers

Imagine you are about to go on your very first flight. You have never stepped foot on a plane before and are beyond nervous. You're scared. You are sitting there anxiously anticipating the flight, and you want to know what to do. You ask everyone around you for advice. Your mom, auntie, cousins, and anyone you know who might know more about planes than you because all you want is to be prepared for what happens next. From what little you know and what you have gathered thus far, surprises, when it comes to planes, are never a good thing, and you want to know what to expect. All you're thinking about is the many stories, movies or even YouTube videos that you've seen of planes that have either crashed or had to make an emergency landing.

This whirlwind of "what if," is overshadowing what really is happening at this very moment. The opportunity and privilege you have to be taking flight in the first place. The day finally comes. Today is the day you take your first flight. You wake up early, head to the airport, and you get there, and you find out you're not even traveling alone. A companion passenger has been assigned to you and to your surprise, you feel so comforted because now you know that you don't have to do this alone. Suddenly this person, this companion, is with you. They're here by your side, not to be overbearing or even to tell you what to do. They're here to make sure that you have someone that understands the process, someone that you can lean on who can help guide you through this new and frightening experience. They allow you to navigate the airport, explaining the many rules of TSA. Empty your pockets. Take your shoes off. Walk through the scanner. Then, as you continue to go through the motions, you feel relief that you are not experiencing this alone. You keep on past security and hop on your airport shuttle headed to your terminal. Finally, you have made it and can start walking towards your gate. You board, nervously locating your seat, and you notice that your companion never left your side the whole time. Your whole ride and the other parent hadn't said a word to you and you're safely positioned on your first flight. When the flight lands, you head to baggage claim. As you collect your luggage, you realize that you didn't need all the extra stuff you packed for the inflight experience. You came prepared with different snacks, pillows, blankets, and books you didn't even need. After claiming everything, your companion looks over at you and says, "let's do this." That is what it feels like to have someone guide you to the next level. Congratulations, you have entered into the next season, chapter and level of what you deserve letting go of all of the feelings of doubt.

I am Tanya Sanders Kelker, and once upon a time, I was you. I sought security in overpreparation. I knew I was ready to take things to the next level, yet I became obsessed with studying and the process of preparation, still leaving me with the feeling of being stuck and lack of fulfillment. My problem wasn't that I didn't know what to do. My problem was that in my mission to be prepared, I had done so much research; what I was experiencing was an information overload. I knew what to do, but I had no idea how. It was tough to strike a balance between listening to myself and listening to others. I was constantly second-guessing myself and my next move, which made me feel like everyone else was correct in what they thought my next steps should be. This cycle of questioning, searching and contemplating fueled my need to hoard knowledge and all the other things that I thought were helping me to become more prepared. I realized that I had gotten so busy looking at others that I was studying their level instead of my own. I was so busy trying to look like, sound like, and walk like someone else's level that it kept me from achieving my next level. Therein lies the problem. You are trying to perfect someone else's game rather than playing your own. You allow yourself to become distracted, and you sacrifice your authenticity. Trust me when I say, know what this looks like. I know what this feels like. And to let you in on a secret, I think it right now, even as I write this book.

In this book, I want to help you navigate the terrains of trials so that you can turn your information into action all while propelling you forward into purpose. I want to help you avoid the same mistakes I made so that you not only have the chance to go further than you would have otherwise but further than I ever could and in a fraction of the time. My dream is for you to be great. I want this experience to help you stand in your power, have confidence in your authority, and take pride in who you are 100% of the way. People often say, "You aren't a leader, unless you have made leaders." Well, I am a leader and my objective as you are reading through these pages is to help you discover untapped potential that will unlock limitless growth and freedom in your life. This is not just another book. This is you finally giving yourself permission to want more for your life, to take everything to the next level, to dream big, to have a vision, to take action, and to transform your life for the better.

Choosing Your Destination

Before we can reach any objective, it is important to first ask ourselves, "Where are we trying to land?" Once we ask ourselves this powerful question, all of the next steps that follow must be intentional, measurable as well as purposeful. There are so many destinations that you could end up in life, whether you are traveling for pleasure or traveling intrinsically for purpose; it is important that if you are struggling with the idea of "where do I go next," that you follow the three steps below to help you navigate where your next step lands.

Spinning The Globe

100 years ago man never thought it was possible to travel as far as the Moon and in the year 2022 as I write the words through this book; man is in the process of planning travels to Mars. The days of limitless possibility are far from over and the vision that you continue to see over and over in your head is possible to make a reality. I heard once a story of a couple that on their monthly date nights, they'd close their eyes, spin the globe and and wherever their finger would end up once the globe stopped spinning; that's where they would book

travel to do dinner next. Now not all of us have the ability to spin the globe and book travel anywhere at any time at this current moment, but I want you to stop allowing your current strength to minimize your ability to create consistent efforts towards your future success. Your circumstance is only limited by your perspective and the first step to choosing your destination is to close your eyes, spin all of the visions around in your mind that you see in your mind, and the first one that you are lead to most is where your next set of actions, commitments and choices should be committed to.

Declaring The Date

Seeing a vision and mentioning it verbally isn't enough to help guide intentional action into realizing it. Once we've identified the next destination it is important for us to choose the date that we'd like to arrive and what airport we are departing from. Our airport departure is our current circumstance and before we can put together the best flight plan that will get us to where we desire, it is important for us to understand what are the factors that are serving as distractions, dividers, or even destroyers towards where we are destined to land. It is more important for you to ask yourself, "where am I?," rather than "where am I going," because if you're not mindful of the factors that caused you to be where you are now, those may be the same viruses that don't allow you to ever end up where you are designed to be.

Measuring The Cost

The cost of your travel will be determined by so many different factors. The departure city and where you are arriving, the days in which you are traveling, the time in which you are departing and various other factors that are considered. When we are looking at landing at our destination of destiny the same factors apply and would be broken up into three categories: environment, discipline, the date you are trying to achieve your goals. The environment that you are in now, will be a major factor that will determine where you are going to travel.

Do the people around you embody the resources, skills and relationships to help accelerate you to where you desire to be? If not, then wouldn't it reduce the learning curve, time and even stress if you entered into an environment that possessed the very things that you desired to have in the future? It is important that who you are around now embodies who you desire to be in the future. These people are necessary to hold you accountable on the days that you are not feeling motivated, responsible to help you navigate the hurdles that may come up in your journey or even available to support you in the times that you may need someone to empathize with where you are in your journey. Once you've understood the importance of the relationships that surround you, I'd implore you to focus on the characteristics inside of you. But the reality of this journey of becoming successful is that during the process, you're not always going to feel motivated. You're not always going to have that immediate inspiration when you wake up in the morning after a hard day's work. You had to deal with your children. You had to drop them off at school and you still are knocked in the face with life's challenges. When motivation doesn't exist, discipline is nec-essary and required to be able to help you reach your destiny. What are the daily activities that you are going to commit to on a daily basis that are going to help you become a champion? Whether that is working out, praying, meditating, or committing to yourself on a daily basis, whether it be taking walks throughout the day, it is important that you create a consistent system that allows you to design an environment that promotes success.

When you're thinking about the date, that you would want to achieve anything, whether it is going on an airplane or if you are trying to fly out tomorrow, it's going to be a bit more expensive and costly than if you are booking travel for about six to nine months from now. It is the same when we're talking about success and trying to be successful as we're measuring the costs. I want you to think about realistic expectations and goals that you may have and not create deadlines and give yourself dates and timelines that are going to stress you out and add more cost to what you're trying to accomplish. It is okay to push things back. But it is not okay to procrastinate in the book balance by Turay Roberts he gives three things to consider when you are trying to reach optimal performance. Three questions to consider are what is my priority? What can wait and what can be delegated? When you are measuring the cost? I want you to consider these three questions every single time and understand what are the things that need to wait. What are the things that can be potentially delegated? Or what are the priorities that I need to focus on right now.

Readying Yourself For Take Off

On every flight, it is important for the flight attendants as well as the passengers to prepare themselves for the takeoff. When we are preparing ourselves for taking off from any-where within our lives, it's important for us to first put our seatbelts on, raise our tray tables and sit our seats forward. And if you're lucky enough to have an exit row and have the privilege of having a bit more leg space, you have to give a verbal confirmation before the plane can actually take off that you are equipped and willing to assist in the case of an emergency. When we think about reading our lives for taking off, there are three critical steps that I want us to consider throughout the rest of this chapter. That will guide the rest of this book and the following pages that you read.

Identifying Your Seat (Know Your Gift)

Number one is to identify your seat when we are identifying our seat on the plane, it's been given to us or chosen for us before we even walk onto the plane. I look at this and identify this is our gift because we were all born with something special. Whether it's a special sauce or an ingredient that makes us who we are. And it is important before we step on our plane towards purpose before we can get to that destination.

It is important for us to understand our gift so that we can position ourselves with the right seat around the right people and be able to lock ourselves in and understand why we were put here a lot of people go their whole lives without understanding why they were put in those seats, why they got those opportunities, or why blessings continue to fall upon them without giving credit to a higher power before you continue to move forward. In your life. I implore you to ask yourself, what were you put in life to do? Who were you put on this world to impact and where were you put on this world to make a difference? What is that burning desire that you have in your heart? What are those creative ideas that you continue to think of? Ask yourself the question of what do I do naturally? Well, what comes easy to me or what are the things that I know to be true? But I'm not putting my best foot forward in trying to accomplish them.

Forming Your Connections (Commit to The Grind)

The right relationships are worth much more than currency in today's society, and as you sit down in your seat on your plane and identify your gift in life, it's important and critical for you to form the necessary connections that embody the principles, the values, the resources and the skill sets that can propel you towards your purpose. As you are focusing on reaching your destination, it is important to have a tribe of individuals that are like minded, goal oriented, self motivated and can inspire, motivate and support you towards where you're going and not exposing where you currently are. Yes, it's important to have people that challenge your current behaviors, habits, or even some of your choices that you make. But it's more important to have people that inspire you to change internally, so that you can become the inspiration that you were destined to become as you are committing to your process. The grind of being able to cultivate inclusive relationships that are reciprocal in today's society is challenging. But this is where it's important for you to use your discernment. Use that gut feeling inside of you and take time to assess the relationships around you so that you can ensure that these people are equipped to pour inside of you. As you form the necessary connections. Ask the right questions and build the right relationships. This will serve as the currency that will get you into any door in the future.

Trusting The Process (Know and Trust in God)

There have not been many flights that I have been on where I have known the pilot that will be flying us to our specific destination. And there might not be many flights that you get on in your lifetime where you know the specific pilot and have a great relationship with this individual based upon previous conversations, and interactions, or even engagements that you may have had. The same is true in life. We don't know the pilot of our life, but it's important for us to build a relationship with a higher power so that we can be held accountable for our actions. Have a belief system and values that are driving our decisions, and have a full commitment to the purpose that we were put on this earth to create and live out because the real question is if we don't reach our purpose, how many others are negatively impacted, and won't be able to reach their own. We have the strength, the capability and all of the resources that we need. Internally we were given all the strength, the knowledge and the skill sets necessary to see us through this journey towards success. It's important for you as you're reading your plane for takeoff to know and trust in a higher power, whatever that is. So that that can be the guiding pilot towards your purpose.

Preparing For Your Landing

At the beginning of almost everything, you are excited, equipped, inspired and motivated to start the race. And as you are preparing yourself to take off, there are so many emotions that sometimes overshadow the logistics in the true skill set to withstand any storm, technical glitch, or any challenge that may arise in life preparing yourself for the landing is much more critical than readying yourself for the takeoff. And a lot of us start races or journeys so fast with excitement and grit, full of life. But as we're going through our journey through this process that we are calling purpose. We encounter many challenges, trials and tribulations that may divert our plane in the air. force us to take emergency landings and it's not about how we navigate the journey. It's more important on how our character allows us to complete the journey as we're preparing ourselves for landing. If we're on a plane, the same rules apply when we are reading ourselves for takeoff. It's important to ensure that our seat belts are safely fastened. It's important for us to raise our tray tables and ensure that the technology or any distractions are stowed away properly. In this section, I'm going to give you three more steps to consider as you're preparing for your landing exactly where you want to be. And throughout the rest of this book. These three guiding principles will come up and be sprinkled throughout some of the chapters so that you will always be able to come back to understand the importance and how to navigate storms, how to overcome hurdles and how to turn any mistake into a monument of success.

Notifying Traffic Control

If the pilot of a plane did not communicate with traffic control, as they are making their final descent and coming a bit closer to their arriving airport, it would create many challenges and potential emergency situation for all passengers as well as the pilots that are involved as you are lowering your plane altitude in getting ready to make your final landing it's important that you notify the people in your life that matter and tell these people the journey that you are getting ready to go on so that it can do two things which are holding you accountable, as well as set the necessary boundaries so that you can not have the distractions that may have once plagued your productivity. It's important for you to communicate your needs and your wants. What are the different things that you require from the people in your life and how can you support them? What do you have the capacity or the ability to do as well as how can they support you throughout the season that you're getting ready to embark on throughout my journey Well, it was always challenging for me to ask for the necessary help when needed. So I want at the beginning of this chapter, before you begin to read the rest of the book, for you to write down three to five things that you need at the end. of this chapter. And who are people in your life that you can go to those people that you can get those things from? Think about the things that you will need not when you are where you are now, but as you get closer to where you are desiring to be. Think about those needs more than the needs that you have right now. Communicate frequently, implement temperature checks, and ensure that people in your life are able to support you throughout this new journey that you are embarking on and that you are capable of receiving support through this new season.

Lowering Your Landing Gear

Like the excitement that goes through my body every time I am sitting on a plane, and I hear the landing gear coming down is such an amazing feeling. It's an amazing feeling for you as you get closer and closer to your destination and the purpose that you've worked so hard to be able to create throughout your life. Throughout this book, I'm going to help you get to that purpose. I'm going to help you identify the goals, the skills, as well as the gift that you have that will be guiding the rest of your life. But one thing that I want you to consider before you continue through the pages of these chapters, is that as you are lowering your landing gear, I want you to ease into it. The landing is all about being smooth, patient and not having a hard landing that will potentially cause the passengers sickness or the plane to be beat up in the process. Remember, this process and journey that we are on is not the end. It is always a new beginning. And every time I plane lands, it needs time to take a break, refuel and then you will be right back in the air in no time moving towards a new destination. Just because you have reached your first destination does not mean that as the last destination so you want to be able to take care of your aircraft or your body or your mind throughout this process. So as you are lowering your landing gear and getting closer to your final descent Don't skip steps in between. Because sometimes those steps can cost you much more than it took you to be able to get to where you are in these clothes. Remember preparing yourself for landing is much more critical than readying yourself for the takeoff because we did not work this hard to have an emergency landing.

Trusting Your Training

You know, there's a quote that I read years ago that stated Be yourself. Everyone else is already taken. And it is important as we're stepping into the season of preparing for our landing, that you trust yourself through this process so that you can soon know how to live. When we begin to find that secret of self trust and not self doubt, we will begin to run our own race in stride, through the seasons of success, understanding that we are equipped, prepared and capable of accomplishing all of the things that we have dreamed of accomplishing our whole lives. You are here reading this book right now, navigating through these chapters, navigating through these pages, reading the words and taking notes and leveraging your highlighter in this moment, to be able to bring attention to the things that you deem as important. But just as you bring attention to the things that you deem as important, I want you to also bring attention to yourself because you are the most valuable and important asset in your life. I want you to trust yourself throughout this process. Trust that you are already equipped, that you've already prepared and that you already have everything that you need throughout this life to be able to guide you to exactly where you want to be. Never trust your fears. They don't know your strength. Trust yourself. You know more than you think you do. And you have more inside of you that you haven't even tapped into yet. Remember as you are coming closer to your landing as you're navigating the pages of this book. Remember you have already been granted permission on purpose. It isn't about you just taking your first step. I am so excited to meet you in the first chapter. And good luck on your journey.

Feelings, Reflections and Actions

Use the pages below to write your feelings or reflections from the chapter or take this time to write out your action plan to begin YOUR BECOMING JOURNEY.

_____

_____

_____

_____

_____

_____

_____

_____

_____

_____

_____

_____

_____

_____

_____

_____

_____

_____

_____

_____

_____

_____

_____

_____

_____

_____

_____

_____

_____

_____

_____

_____

_____

TANYA KELKER

Chapter 1

WHO ARE YOU, REALLY?

"Success is only meaningful and enjoyable if it feels like your own." - Michelle Obama

Why in the history of interviewing is the question, "tell me about yourself," the hardest question to answer? For the last 20, 30 or however many years you've been alive, you've been experiencing your life better than anyone else, yet this is the absolute hardest question for you to answer. Is that we don't know the proper technique to answer this loaded question, or is that truly, we don't believe that our experiences, contributions and ability to overcome challenges thus far in life aren't significant enough to win the role that we may be auditioning for.

Similar in life, when people ask who we are or what we do our response is typically a title. We say things like, "Oh I'm a mom", "oh I'm a teacher", or "oh I'm a doctor". Rarely do we ever describe who we are as a person and to me, that's really where the challenge arises. When someone asks who we are, the answer is that we are people. As people, we are designed to be something not simply to do something. If our sole purpose was to do something that would make us machines. Somehow, we have developed a culture that dictates who we are by being defined by what we do. That's a huge misconception that in this chapter, we will debunk as well as help you better understand who you are, why you are here, and how you too are significant.

The 5 Questions That Matter Most

If we don't know ourselves because simply we don't ask ourselves greater questions we don't sit and think with ourselves enough in a room in solitude or at a park, or in a place where it's silent of all of the noise around us. We are often consumed by work, technology, social media, and relation-ships are the different hats that we wear. So we attach our identity to all of these other meaningless things, rather than finding the meaning in ourselves. So before you can really be able to understand your contribution, your significance and your influence on the world or the people around you whether it be your family, your workplace, or your commu-nity. You have to start asking yourself better questions and being willing to hear the answer and be accepting of where you are in that current moment before we can get to the place of where we want to be in life in the future. We have to come to grips and be accepting without shame of where we are right now. A lot of us don't face who we are when we look in the mirror and it creates an unhealthy relationship with ourselves because then when other people challenge our current actions, choices or decisions that may not directly align with what we communicate to people that we are, then we feel offended. But rather, they are just mirrors of what we need to see. Or the things that we see within ourselves that we don't appreciate. We don't value or try to hide from the world. I challenge you to think about prior to answering the questions below. What are the secrets that you don't want anybody to find out about who you truly are at the core? And if someone knew the things that you hid from the world, would they still feel the same way about you? Would you still have the same influence that you do that they do not see the secrets? Before you can move forward throughout this chapter and throughout the rest of the book? I wanted to provide you five guiding questions that I believe matter most, that will help you get a full picture and an understanding on who you are now. What are the things that are important to you? What is the story that is shaping your life? What is the story that you have been telling yourself your whole life? And what are the values at the core of who you are, that maybe are creating your decisions, your choices, being the foundation to the relationships that you create, and helping you understand what you see is most valuable in your life. Again, before we can move forward, we must pull the curtain back on where we are, unpack our baggage before we're able to move forward into our new destination.

The Questions to Guide Who You Are

- If money wasn't an option and your bills were going to be paid forever, what would you be actively doing in life?

- What is the story in your life that best represents who you are now?

- If you were accepted, loved and valued by everyone you came in contact with, describe who you would be.

- What is the part of your life that you wish you were able to share with the world more?

- What are the things that you value the most in life?

Getting to Know Yourself

The question, "Who am I," may be one of the most challenging questions to answer and could bring up a series of questions, emotions, thoughts and feelings that you may not be ready for. That feeling of loss or confusion when working to understand who we are as individuals is normal and so many individuals experience a blank stare when asked that question. If you were to not use any titles or accolades, who would you desire to be in the present moment? I want you to commit to the three steps below so you can be more confident the next time you're challenged to answer the question, "who am I?"

Recognize Who You Don't Want to Be

I am in agreement with you if you believe that identifying who you are may be challenging and identifying the things that you want may be a process that we're not ready to go through if we haven't went through a series of maybe trauma, unpacking, or potential therapy that has allowed us to really reflect on where we are, who we are and what we really desire in life. I still believe that one of the most challenging questions that we encounter is when people ask us what we want to eat, whether it be for dinner, lunch, or for breakfast in the morning, because there's so many options. There's so many different places that you can go, cuisines that you can eat or recipes that you would want to be able to create. But identifying that one thing similar to in life is very challenging to isolate what that one thing would be. And oftentimes, when someone then gives us ideas and starts to mention potential food ideas or restaurants, we often go to what we don't want and there's a lot of ones that come up prior to the yes of choosing that restaurant, that meal or that place that you may decide on. I believe that the same process is true within life. And that we recognize through our journey of becoming that we're going to run into a lot more nose than eyes. We're going to maybe have challenging relationships and those challenging relationships will help us find the one for us. We may have a lot of jobs or internships that we don't necessarily desire. But it leads us to having the job that is in our mind, our dream job, and then anything in life. It's important for us to not allow the initial knowledge to discourage us from continuing to keep pushing forward. As you are getting to know yourself. The first step is to recognize who you don't want to be and write down the characteristics the things and potential choices and behaviors of the person that you may have been at one period of time, or you may be now that you don't want to be and then reverse engineer the intentions, the steps, the choices that are important, the environment that this person would have to be around. So that you can then become the person that you desire. So the best way to first become the person that you want is to understand what you don't want

Connecting Purpose to Passions

one of the worst questions that I believe teachers, parents and adults, as children, as they are growing up is what do they want to be when they grow up? Rather, I implore you and challenge you as children or our youth as well as yourself. Who do you want to be and what do you want to create as you grow older? It's important for us as we're growing older, and identifying the different characteristics that will help us become the person that we actually desire. And this process of getting to know ourselves to connect our future with purpose and passions, rather than connecting it with a profession. When we isolate our minds, and centralize it on professions and job titles, then that's what we identify ourselves with. To become. But with if we operate more in a fluid way, and our creations and our innovations and our different things that we engage with from a passions or interests, then it will allow us to open up opportunities for us to learn for us to engage or for us to be exposed to different things that may not necessarily be what society sees it successful. But as we are engaging in it, we see ourselves as happy when we begin to connect our purpose with our passions. I'd be happy that it sets up the roadmap and a step by step process to living a life of fulfillment. Success, by definition, in my opinion, is fulfillment and freedom of choice and action. I believe that we have looked at success as the ability to have wealth, the ability to have influence as well as the ability to be seen as successful. And there's a lot of people throughout my career in the past as well as now that are not successful. And there may be some of the wealthiest people, but they are empty and find themselves bankrupt often within themselves. Before we can really identify this idea of success I want you to first identify what are you passionate about? What are the things that you enjoy doing and enjoy talking about the different activities that you feel free and that you feel that the world has stopped when you're engaging with them? What are some of the topics that you enjoy talking about? Whether it be with colleagues, friends, family members are the things that you defend without even knowing it? What are the things that make you smile? Feel a sense of joy and peace within yourself when you're actively doing them? And when you begin to reflect as a part of this process of getting to know yourself on the things that you're already doing? I believe it creates a roadmap and a blueprint for all of the things that you're already doing that you should be doing on a daily basis. If you just begin to put those things in your daily activity. As a part of getting to know yourself, I want you to write down three to five things today that you've done with them in the last two to three weeks that have really made you happy. And then I want you to ask yourself if you could get paid for doing those things. Would you stop what you're doing now? And continue to do those things for the rest of your life? If it's yes, then my question for you is what is stopping you? If it is no, then I implore you to continue to find things that make you feel these feelings that you desire, and continuing to put those in your daily activity so that you can always have a sense of peace, joy, and allow passions to power up your day on your pursuit to purpose

Trust What Your Heart is Communicating

Trusting yourself is one of the most challenging things to do and commit to on a daily basis. Trusting what your heart is communicating to you is even more challenging because it takes a level of intentionality. It takes a deeper level of listening and it takes silence internally as well as around you. And in today's world of technology, and a world that's full of distractions, and things pulling you in 1000 directions, it's hard for us to find those places when we are silent. And when we are able to disconnect fully from the world around us. Bill Gates, Steve Jobs, Warren Buffett, and some of the most wealthy people that have ever lived, but also some of the most innovative people that have ever lived, took weeks of not vacation, but opportunities to think they would call it thinking time and Michael burn off in his book average sucks. Talked about what he did on his thinking weeks, where whether it'd be a day, a weekend, or if you had the opportunity of taking a week off that they would travel to a specific location around the world and leave their technology, their phones, their laptops, their computers, and simply just take a pencil, paper and their mind and have the opportunity of silencing everything around them and thinking about the things that they want to do. Thinking about the world around them, thinking about what they're feeling, and how innovations can be created. If you took time every day to think about ideas for 30 minutes a day, it would be five ideas created on a daily basis. By the end of the year you would have 1000s of ideas that you would be able to say that you've created and the reality of it is of these 1000 ideas all it takes is one to be cutting edge innovative in something that can change the world. The reason that we are not in the positions that we had been called to be in is that we're not taking enough time sitting down, silencing our mind, silencing our body and thinking about the things that are going on inside of us that are going on around us. As well as thinking about the things that we would want to create in the future as well as in the present. As you are getting to know yourself. It is important to listen to yourself and trust what your heart is communicating. True freedom is the bridge between what we truly want and what God has in store for us. And as we walk across that bridge between our wants and desires, and his wants and desires. It is important for us to follow the urges of our hearts so that we can be able to navigate the terrains of trials and tribulations so that we can make it across this bridge and enter into a place of purpose.

Documenting Your Thoughts and Discoveries

What have you discovered lately about yourself about how you think, how you perceive the world? And are those perceptions of the world and of yourself, influencing your actions and your decisions? When we begin to document our thoughts, our discoveries, our interactions or engagements, or even the things that we're exposing ourselves to on a daily basis, it helps us create a full picture and a canvas of who we actually are. And if we think about our actions over the last seven to 10 days does it directly align with who we say we're trying to become in the future? I believe that activity doesn't equal achievement, but activity tells us a picture and tells us a story on what we actually care about. And if you were to assess your activity over the last month, does your activity directly align with the vision that you've been praying about? Working towards and communicating to people that you were committed to? So often in my own life, I recognize that my work had consumed me to a point that wasn't helping me work towards my purpose and my overall desire in life. And if you are anything like me, and your work has consumed you, and you haven't had time to write that book, build that business, start that nonprofit and go serve in your community. Then it's time to take time documenting your actions, your thoughts and your discoveries and ask yourself why those things are in the way of the thing that you've been called to do. The often response that I get is finances, bills and certain responsibilities have to be taken care of. The path of self discovery of thought, action and habit is our first step of putting us back on the road of success. How can you use your gift and skill set to assist you with taking care of your certain responsibilities? What have you discovered about your belief system that may be influencing you to take action in building a business or taking advantage of opportunities that have been awaiting your attention? Before we can walk into our calling it is up to us to use our gifts to remove us from our circumstances.

Identify Crisis

There is a considerable difference between the person people think you are, the person people say you are, and who you are. This means that you have to know who you are. I used to own a spa where I was the CEO, manager, and service provider. In addition to wearing my many spa hats, I was a coach to other aspiring spa professionals. I was trying to do everything at once. Why? I hadn't yet taken the time to understand who I was outside of the title that my position held. During this period, I managed to injure my back, forcing me to take a step back because there were certain things I couldn't do anymore. I could no longer wear many of the hats that came with working in the spa and had to shift to coaching full-time. During this time, outside of being a mom and a wife, nothing felt right to me, and I was forced to evaluate who I was and who I wanted to be. I realized that through all of it, I was only working these jobs and holding these positions because they were paying the bills. So, I continued to do them anyway, even though the work made me extremely unhappy. I was good at what I did, which is why I initially chose to enter the field; however, my clients could see through the facade, which eventually made them unhappy.

During this time, I also realized that I loved helping my clients build their businesses more than I enjoyed helping them with their accounting. Coming to this realization was challenging, especially since I had to invest time and money in going to school for accounting. It was even harder coming to this understanding at a time when I could no longer perform spa services. Everyone told me to revisit my plan B, the thing I got my degree in, accounting. Through it all, I learned the importance of being okay with who I am. I learned to love and forgive myself for things I couldn't control. I learned to stop listening to the distracting opinions of others and to focus on myself. At this point in my journey, it was imperative that I both understand and embrace the light, energy, and power that rested in fully accepting who I was. As you are joining through your journey, I want you to understand where are the sources of your pain and if they are in your work, in your home, or even in your own perspectives and beliefs, that it is time to make a shift and change. At the beginning, like for me, it will feel uncomfortable and you will wake up some mornings and just want to cry, but I can assure you that the tears will wash away who you weren't so you can become who you are meant to be. Here are two things to consider as you are creating the identity that you are proud of.

Looking Inward and Explore Deep

Sometimes the most simple solution to life's problems starts with self examination and being able to understand and discover yourself at a deeper level. As you're getting to know yourself, and recreating the identity that has existed for so long that you may not be very happy about. It's important that you look inward and explore deep down and this takes a level of patience, intentionality, as well as vulnerability. That you will create another level of courage and commitment, commitment to yourself growth as you are getting to know yourself better. It's important for you to ask yourself, what makes this decision challenging? What are the things about yourself that you love, or potentially aren't very proud of?

What are the limits and boundaries that you haven't set within people's relationships in your life? And what are areas that you would want to improve? What are the stories behind your perspectives and where those come from? And are they perspectives that are even your own? A lot of us navigate life believing that our stories are filled with trauma, baggage, or even all of these negative perspectives that shape our current reality whereas we've really taken on the baggage of our parents, the baggage of the people or the colleagues that we may work with. Sometimes we even take on the perspectives or baggage of the person that we say that we're in love with. So through this process of self examination, this is the time where you like any examination in school, take yourself through a list of questions and considerations, so that you can really explore yourself at a deeper level and ask why to all of the things that you're experiencing and feeling. I heard a quote that said velocity is created through vulnerability. And it's important for you to be vulnerable so that you could be able to move forward throughout your life and the way that you actually once before we can identify the person that we want to be.

We have to understand who we currently are. We have to understand the perspectives, the thoughts, the choices that we have to pull out in the weeds that we have to pull up in order to plant the right perspectives and the seeds of success that can continue to push us and move us forward.

Set Your Sail Towards Joy

The truth is choosing joy each day has nothing to do with how we feel about our present circumstance or what's even going on in our lives. It's really about what we are going to do and the actions that follow in spite of all of these feelings that we feel and the circumstances that currently exist around us. It's really being able to say that I don't have the necessary finances, but I'm going to go find an audio book for free to learn how to take me out of my current circumstance. It's saying that despite of my heartbreak from the relationship that I thought was everything, that I'm still going to allow myself to be open to love, and take my time through this process to find the best person that's meant for me understanding how to be joyful in the midst of crisis takes a level of belief, faith, as well as humility and courage that is necessary as a part of this journey. Being able to commit to affirming yourself, even when we feel like our sail or our ship isn't advancing forward is important. So we have to ensure that we have daily activities in our lives that are critical, and that are committed on a daily basis that will drive and continue to set our sail towards joy. I want you to think about all of the ways to fill your day with joy. Whether that's communicating to a friend that always makes you laugh, listening to a specific audio book that always brings you inspiration, or listening to a specific song that just continues to uplift you every day. Whatever the things are, in your life that you need. You have to ensure that you are putting those into your calendar on a daily basis. We fill our calendars with meetings with responsibilities with all of the things that we have to do for work, but we sometimes forget often about eating, about taking a walk around our park, about sitting on our porch and just looking at the trees blow in the wind, or about taking time to potentially think we have to choose joy and every situation and allow that to be what is poured into us through the resources and through the assets that continue to guide our life so that we can ensure that we're choosing to pour it out into the world around us. Joy is a perspective, it's a state of mind and what we think about our perspective, our circumstance, and our current position within our life will continue to guide how we treat ourselves throughout this process. Remember, as we are continuing to shift this identity remember to set your sail towards Joy, choose it on a daily basis, despite any challenge that you're experiencing, and make it a part of your daily ritual.

Confront, Forgive, Know, and Accept Yourself

You can't be afraid of who you are when you are by yourself. Being alone allows you to test yourself. It's almost like studying for a test. You're doing all the studying, but won't know its accuracy until the test is in front of you. Without testing yourself at each checkpoint how do you know you are ready to move on to the next level? Some people are on the right track and searching for motivation. Others are unsure of what is next and need little guidance. Yet both understand that something has to change to achieve elevation. Once you have successfully gone through the confrontation, forgiving, and accepting, you will be able to know who you are In Christ.

Silencing The Negative Critic {You}

The moment you realize that you are the biggest critic that is causing your destruction and your division from your destiny. At that same time, it's time for you to silence them. Self- talk is common amongst most people and some is positive, uplifting, inspirational. But oftentimes the other side of self-talk can be damaging and detrimental and can destroy the very things of beauty that you have inside of you. It's important to focus with intentionality to eliminate and extinguish all of the self-defeating dialog that has a negative impact on the next steps that will guide who you are designed to be in every time that you believe that something negative is inside of your mind. I want you to begin to write it down. Similar to how we talked about in previous chapters, it's important that you document your thoughts and the discoveries but it's also important that you document the different perspectives that aren't necessarily moving you closer to your goal and can be potentially pulling you away from your goals. It's important that you begin with what you're actually thankful for. Write down the list of limiting beliefs as well as all of the opportunities of gratitude that can potentially overshadow all of the things that you may feel in that current moment. And it's important in this time that you're reflecting on all of this negative self talk, that you feel what you are feeling, but you also tell whatever it is that you believe to stop and that it's time to introduce affirmations in place of criticism that you would continue to take yourself through when you are feeling down and you don't want to work. Affirm yourself. When you are not wanting to continue to move forward and you're wanting to quit, it's time for you to affirm yourself. And the best way of recreating your thought process is being in an environment of positivity. So think about the people around you, think about the relationships that you have. And think about what type of music you're listening to all of the different things that you expose yourself to and ask yourself do any of those things around you have an influence on how you currently think? Think about where you want to be much more than where you currently are. And sometimes this process takes closing your eyes and creating a mental image of yourself in a place removed from any limiting belief. I want you to focus on your surroundings, who is around you and how you feel during this current space. And the more that you replace all of the self criticism. With self empowerment, you will look up one day and be exactly the person that you visualize yourself to be through those challenges.

View Each Loss as a Lesson For Growth

One of my favorite quotes regarding failure comes from Michael Jordan years ago, who said I've missed more than 9000 shots in my career. I've lost almost 300 games 26 times. I've been trusted to take the game winning shot and missed. I failed over and over again in my life. And that's why it succeeded. Every single opportunity that you have to go through life is just that, an opportunity and we have to stop looking at losses in our life because there are lessons to continue to get better. Whether or not you close that sales deal you could learn from that potential client. Whether or not you got that house that you wanted. You can learn more about the real estate process and whether or not that relationship worked out, you know, what potentially is necessary and what you could have done differently so that the next relationship could be the best for you. We do not learn from the times that we have one. We learn more from the times that we have lost so it's important for us to own the mistakes or even the challenges that we experience and begin to dissect all of the different things that may be we could have done better or could have been different so that it could have produced a different outcome. If you are not failing, then you're not learning. And it's important for us to understand that failure is a necessary step to the road towards progress. And it is a part of a journey that will not settle for stagnation. If you want to continue to move forward in your life in your journey, and continue to move forward in becoming the person that you choose to be. Then you're going to fail as a part of this process. You're going to get things wrong, but I guarantee if you continue to commit to this process that we have explored throughout the rest of this book throughout our time together you will understand who you are, have the techniques to navigate life's storms and be proud of the person that you chose to design.

Chapter Success Strategy

Activity/Exercise:

- Write Out Things that you think about yourself

- Write out things that other people say about you

- Then review and reflect if you agree or disagree with this

- You can't confront it if you don't write it down and see it

- How do you feel about the results?

- What would they change or what would you want to add to this?

Feelings, Reflections and Actions

Use the pages below to write your feelings or reflections from the chapter or take this time to write out your action plan to begin YOUR BECOMING JOURNEY.

_____

_____

_____

_____

_____

_____

_____

_____

_____

_____

_____

_____

_____

_____

_____

_____

_____

_____

_____

_____

_____

_____

_____

_____

_____

_____

_____

_____

_____

_____

_____

_____

_____

Chapter 2

DESIGNING THE LIFE YOU ENVISION

"How far are you willing to go to create the life you want?" - Gina Greenlee

I n chapter one, we walked you through discerning who you are while exploring the recipe that will help you find that person that you deeply desire to be. In this chapter we are exploring what you deeply desire and what steps to put in place in order to acquire that. You have the power and authority to ask for anything you desire. The tricky part is being able to identify what you want and why. Not too long ago, I went to a conference where a lady was speaking; she opened her presentation by asking the audience, what do you want? She went around the room and asked everyone what they wanted, and the responses were vague, generic, and very surface-level. Then she said, "Okay, everyone. I hear you offering solutions to the things that you're looking for. But what do you want?". She looked me dead in the eyes and said, *"So you pay all this money to come and listen to get more information just to have a course? You get a course, then what? What are you here for? Why are you here?"*.

That moment shook something in me because it was the moment that I realized she was right. I didn't need more information on how to do anything else. I was there for a reason. She had what I needed and all I had to do was tell her what I wanted to get it. The problem was that I wasn't clear on exactly what I wanted at the time. This is true for most of us in life and business when we are on the journey to the next level. So to avoid you going through that, I want you to write down your goal. This is your big picture.

When using a GPS for guidance, there are a few essential pieces of information you must have. First, you have to have a starting point. This is where you are currently, your starting position. Second, you need to have your desired address. This is your goal or final destination, and the GPS will give you different routes to your last location.

My Biggest Goal is to

_____

_____

_____

My Current Position Is

_____

_____

_____

The First 7 Turns (Steps) That I Have to Make Are

_____

_____

_____

In this exercise above, I want you to be super clear on where you want to go, where you currently are and the steps necessary to get to that specific position. Once you finish completing this activity, I want you to commit to putting a big "x" through all of what you wrote because through this chapter we are erasing all of the limitations that you've set for yourself and exposing you to what is possible in your life if you continue to believe in the possible.

In this chapter you will learn our step by step method on assessing where you are currently while being able to understand the best course of action moving forward. Oftentimes we are using our current strength for our future aspirations and we believe it just isn't enough. But through the preparation process, you will grow the stamina, strength and understanding on what you need to do and where you need to go, so you can become who you are destined to become. When was the last time you asked the question, "where am I in life right now?" and genuinely had an answer that is honest as well as productive as you map out a plan to get exactly where you are. In this chapter we are going to give you a step by step process on assessing where you are, so that in the next few chapters moving forward you can create a blueprint that will assist you in getting to where you desire to be.

The 5 Questions That Matter Most

Since we were children growing up, we have been hardwired to want to be able to answer questions. But we haven't been truly taught the importance of asking great questions. Even in class, we were taught to raise our hands to ask the professor questions and a lot of times because of the lack thereof, confidence or belief in ourselves, we didn't want to be the outcast and the person that seemed or claimed that they didn't know what was going on. So a lot of times we didn't ask questions that would help us have insight into being able to better help us prepare for our educational endeavors.

The same is true within our lives. We're never taught to ask ourselves questions. We may be the coach or the mentor or the leader in so many different places providing people answers, but when we have to actually implement the information that we've given out to other people to do that sounds great. We're often the amateur or the rookie and are able to implement the same advice that we would give other people. If you want to understand where you want to go in life, we've provided you five questions that would help you navigate your current beliefs, perspective, or even your current circumstance so that you can be able to better navigate and understand what are things that you want, how to assess your goals, what position you want to be within three to five years, as well as the difference that you want to make in the world.

- Five years from now, if everything went exactly the way you wanted, where do you see yourself and with whom would you spend most of your time?

- What are three to five goals that you'd want to accomplish in life that seem impossible?

- When you look forward to the person that you desire to become, how would you describe this person?

- If you can have any five things in life, what would you want and why are those things important to you?

- If you could make a difference in one population of people who would it be and how would you be making a difference?

Silencing The Noise in The Background

In the age of technology we are constantly being interrupted and divided more and more from what we are called to create in the world. Silence and solitude are two things that we just don't get a lot of in our day and age, lacking the margin in our lives that we so desperately need.

Identify the Source of the Noise

Before we can be able to adequately and effectively silence the noise in the background, we have to first identify the source of the noise. It's similar to if you're in your home office at home, and you're trying to read a book or get some work done in this continuous sound that keeps playing in the background that is distracting you from being able to progress forward on that page or on that report that you're trying to finalize.

Until you leave your office. And identify where that noise is coming from, where the sound is coming from. You really can't address it. And sometimes in life, it takes you removing yourself from your current position in order for you to find the source of noise that is stopping you from getting to where you desire and that desired position. That noise may be a family member, that noise may be friends, that noise may be technology or certain distractions. That noise may be certain critics in your head that you are the voices in your head of self limiting beliefs or things that have shaped and shifted your perspective about yourself on a daily basis.

You have to first identify the source of noise by asking yourself where or who or what is causing stress, Tension, friction and anything that is not providing you what it is that you desire or need so that you can continue to progress forward. When we begin to identify the noise, then it's important for us to next identify the course of action to silence the noise whether that is having a crucial conversation with a person that is not not giving you what you need, whether that is setting certain boundaries or creating time on your calendar. To disconnect from it all. It's important to first identify the root cause of where the noise is coming from the overall source. Once you've met the source of the noise in your life, now it's time to take a course of action. And then the third step is to be able to put a system in place so that this noise can not continue to distract you. I truly believe that life doesn't get easier. We just get stronger. And sometimes as we're growing and what we'll learn is as we're trying to become successful and we're working towards that the noise is not going to get any lower in sound or in volume. But we just learned how to put systems in place so that we don't hear or allow them to affect us in the same way.

Physically Disconnect From The World

Disconnecting from the natural world takes intention and courage but will create a sense of peace and clarity that is needed and necessary. For you to be able to cultivate your calling, and take being able to cut the cord of codependency and life we have to learn how to physically disconnect at certain periods of times. I believe with the rise in technology and the access of information, new news, and different things that continue to trigger us to always be connected. It's challenging and sometimes being able to have our thoughts influenced by our own perspectives. But I believe that a few things are important to consider. So that you can be able to disconnect, silence the noise and be able to come one within yourself, whether that is leaving work, to be able to make it a point of relaxing after work hours, whether it's taking a social media detox or engaging in activities without your phone, disconnecting from potential friends or family members that are showcasing toxic behaviors or are not healthy for your specific state of mind or position in which you are going as well as putting all devices away before bed or while you're eating and engaging with people. I think all of these are great displays of disconnecting so that you can be present in the moment. One of the things that we realize is that we're so focused on what's going on around us that we often miss the moments that are happening right there within us. And right there within the relationships that we're having in the conversation that we're currently engaging in, or just in the moment that we're continuing to create. Don't be so focused on the next moment, the future opportunity, or even the future engagement that hasn't happened yet that you continue to miss the moments that you're bypassing. So it's important to disconnect from society. And if you truly want to be removed from society, stop always following what is happening around you. Avoid speaking or communicating to anyone at all, maybe for a period of time, so that you can focus on what it is that you need the questions that you have to ask yourself so that you can be able to listen clearly to what the answers are.

Learn to Listen

I believe that one of the most sincere forms of love and self actualization is actually listening to what you have to say internally. Listening allows us to look within ourselves and become more aware of the barriers that inhibit our ability to listen more effectively. It takes courage, it takes patience, but it also it takes us silencing all of the noise using the strategies listed above, so that we can be able to have a better understanding of where we are, what we desire, empathize with our current position without being shameful, but also give ourselves grace so that we can continue to move forward. Listening isn't just about what's being communicated. It's about what's being received, understood, waited and responded.

You could listen to something being communicated to yourself, but if you're not really taking time to understand what this means, evaluating methods to overcome this thought or this specific feeling as well as responding with more progressive action, then it's not necessarily benefiting you in the way that you would need it to benefit you so that you can continue to progress forward. When we talk about effective listening or in school we always learn about active listening. These different characteristics can help you become a better student of self, so that you can be the leader of people. Learn to listen to what is being communicated throughout your body, the signs of soreness, the signs of stress, the signs of tension within your body are all communicating to you potentially need to slow down to take a break or get some support or assistance in areas that you've been neglecting for some period of time. If we want to be able to silence the noise and have a clear plan on navigating this space of getting everything that you desire. We have to become better listeners of ourselves.

Getting to Know Where You're Going

What do you truly want in your life? If you were granted everything you ever prayed and wished for tomorrow, would you be ready to accept the responsibility that comes with it? I believe that there are two reasons that the majority of people don't get to experience success at the highest level because 1. They don't think about it enough and 2. Once they achieved it, they weren't prepared to sustain it through commitment to the responsibilities that were required.

Becoming Who You Envision

If you were to meet the person that you desire to become 15 years from now, what would that person be like? What would they be wearing? What would be their demeanor? What area of town would they live in? What would be their conversation or the book that they just finished up reading? What would be their daily activity or the clothes that they wear or the different things that potentially interests them? Talk to me a little bit about their relationship with themselves as well. As the relationship with their children or their spouse. What is stopping you from becoming that person right now? In order for us to become the person that we envision the quickest way to becoming that person is to actually act the part of that individual right now. Now, you may not be able to wear the exact clothes and drive the exact car, but what are the characteristics, the values, the work ethic, the interest in the books that this individual reads? What are all of the different things that you can do to be like this person in regards to their demeanor? How can you shape your specific interactions, relationships, as well as become this person intrinsically? So that when you actually do become this person, it's already second nature. And you have to become the person not that you're settling to be now in this current circumstance in the place that you're in. But if you want to actually become the person that you envision, you have to embody those principles, those characteristics, and those actions and decisions now, I think oftentimes we procrastinate. We make decisions or choices based upon where we currently are right now in life. But if we want to be another person, you are capable of being that person right now. The first step to getting to know where you are going, is to become who you envisioned to be. Think of three to five things that this person does, where's the characteristics of that person and commit to yourself starting today, that you're going to start living it now.

Setting an Unreachable Goal and Cutting the Timeline in Half

At the beginning of every year, everyone I believe in the world sets their New Year's resolutions, communicating that they have 12 months to be able to accomplish a specific set of goals that will make them feel successful at the end of year. Most cases, there's financial goals attached to specific people's lives, whether it be to get out of debt, increase their revenue, or put a certain amount of money into savings or investment opportunities. When I think about 12 month goals, I think that there's so much life that can happen within 12 months, that it's almost unrealistic to think that you would be able to commit to these goals for a specific 12 month process. What is one goal that you have that you've set out maybe six to 12 months from now? And what would it take to cut that goal in half to be able to accomplish what it takes a certain amount of money? Would it take a certain amount of resources or people in your life that have that specific skill set? What would it take for you to accomplish your goals in half the time? I want you as you're going through this specific chapter, to flip back a few pages where we made you write down your big goal that you are trying to achieve. And then in that we talked about your current position and what you had readily available. And then also the first seven steps that you had to make in order for you to be able to achieve that big goal. When we wrap it around thinking about that big goal right here. It's important that we understand that it may take us individually 12 months, maybe 24 months to accomplish that big goal with only the resources, the skills and the knowledge or even the access to different things that we have readily available within our lives. But who would you need? What would you need? And where would you need to be so that you could be able to take that goal and chop it in half. I want you to think about three to five different areas that you can consider that would help you accomplish your goal in half the time this specific year, whether it's increasing your finances in 12 months and six months, instead of paying off your debt in six months, do it in three months, instead of building a million dollar company in two years. What would it take for you to do it in one year? I want us to begin setting unreachable goals and cutting the timeline in half.

Focusing on Priorities, Purpose and Productivity

In this journey of becoming successful, there were only three things that matter. The why, the what, and the how, why are you doing what it is that you were wanting to embark on? What are you specifically needing to do to be able to accomplish this journey? As well as how are you going to go about doing the things necessary? The activity, the habits, the choices and the workload, so that you could be able to accomplish this within a given period of time. When we think about this in three words. It measures priorities, purpose, as well as productivity. When we think about our purpose, when is the last time you've asked yourself why do I actually want this? Is it your dream? Or is it a society influenced dream that you've adopted as a part of growing through life? When you think about your specific purpose in life, I don't believe that we've all just been given one purpose. I believe that we've been given one purpose. I believe that we are given one purpose at a time until it is realized. I once heard a quote that said the best funerals to go to are the ones when your dreams die, because you succeeded in achieving them. I believe this is the same when it's true. On purpose. Your next purpose in your life is opened up in your mind once you intentionally accomplish the first person, best that's been put into your mind when we think about the specific priorities. This is really focusing on activity and not achievement and not just doing a lot of activity, like a hamster on a wheel, and really being able to push the needle forward. Being productive is not just doing a lot of work. Being productive means doing the right work that can progress the goal forward in an effective and an efficient way. What are the different things that you need to do as a part of this journey? And how are you committing every single activity on a daily basis to be able to commit and accomplish the very things that you're setting out to accomplish?

Feelings, Reflections and Actions

Use the pages below to write your feelings or reflections from the chapter or take this time to write out your action plan to begin YOUR BECOMING JOURNEY.

_____

_____

_____

_____

_____

_____

_____

_____

_____

_____

_____

_____

_____

_____

_____

_____

_____

_____

_____

_____

_____

_____

_____

_____

_____

_____

_____

_____

_____

_____

_____

Chapter 3

GOOD IDEAS VS. GOD IDEAS

"Man says... show me and I'll trust you. God says... Trust me and I'll show you." - Psalm 126:6

What if the plan that you methodically planned for months or even years goes isn't the one that can push you through the finish line? What happens if you worked your whole career with an intentional focus on becoming a million dollar earner and then you are cursed with the "seven figure" curse leading most black entrepreneurs and professionals to committing suicide. When we think about the desire to wanting to comitt suicide, I believe it is a direct correlation to the lack of alignment spiritually and comes up when our focus is being shifted away from our purpose and towards profits. I never thought this would be my story as well until I found myself in the same situation that so many of my peers experienced.

I began to notice the obsession with making a dollar to the point where I no longer knew what I was destined to become. I was walking blindly into buildings, possessed by profit, attached to accomplishments all while being tangled in toxic work ethic. Once I saw myself in this place I recognized that there was a shift that needed to happen and I had to undergo a pruning process so I could enter a season of evolution and transformation. During this process I found myself sitting and being alone and realized that my current actions, habits and priorities were in direct misalignment with where I believe I was being called to be.

In this chapter you will walk away with an intentional plan on how you navigate the terrain of trials and tribulations so you can transform your mistakes into monuments of success.

Preparing Your Mindset

The only reason you haven't already achieved what you are seeking is because deep down you don't believe you deserve it. We attract only what we "are" in our minds through the way of our actions in life. If we desire an outcome, we must learn how to see it in our minds, become it in our actions so that we can achieve it in our lives. The changing of what you think about it, will produce changes in what you become.

Don't Let Desires Distract You (Opportunities Come in Form of Distraction)

A mentor told me years ago that as you grow be mindful of the distractions that are disguised as opportunities to advance your life. Anything that doesn't directly assist or accelerate you towards the goal you are currently working toward achieving must be seen as a direct interference with your success and must be treated accordingly. In my life as I started to move closer to purpose, distractions stopped looking like "parties," they became networking events. Distractions didn't look like social media, they became "information overload via podcasts or YouTube." Distractions weren't television or Netflix, they became opportunities to "partner or collaborate" on projects that would yield a financial return, but couldn't put me in the position to win in my purpose. Just because it pays you, doesn't mean it won't destroy or distract you. As you continue to grow it's important that you don't let what you desire in the moment distract you from what you are destined to become. Using discernment and measuring each and every opportunity against your open true goal and purpose is necessary and is important in assessing each "opportunity" as they are presented to you.

Defining Your Measurable and Outcome

It is challenging to meet any objective that you haven't created a measurable for. What does success look like if you were to achieve that which you are working so diligently to achieve? How will you know that you've achieved your goal, aspiration and desire if you don't have a clear measurable on what the experience looks like. As you are assessing what you want and setting goals, also note the experience, the feeling and draw out an empathy map of what you would want to experience so that you can create just that. Often, we set only a financial or arbitrary goal that doesn't have the specifics attached to it and when we accomplish it, it doesn't give us the specific feeling that we desire so we feel like we have failed. Follow the model below to measure your goals and measurables moving forward.

When I achieve my goal I will...

Say

_____

_____

_____

Hear

_____

_____

_____

See

_____

_____

_____

Think and Feel

_____

_____

_____

Identify The Responsibility and Master the Accountability

Having goals and dreams is no longer enough and we are not willing to commit to the responsibilities, actions and sacrifices that come with achieving them. In everything we gain, it will take us losing something and I have seen people lose so much as they work to become successful that at the end, they were just left with the number that existed in their bank account. Don't let the pursuit of assets, accomplishments and advancement have you in a place where you have sacrificed all that had access to your heart and spirit. Before we move forward on this journey it is important to ask yourself, what am I willing to GIVE UP in order to GO UP. When you are vulnerable and honest with yourself after this question, this will create limits on what you are willing to do or what you are not willing to do. One of the top financial experts and CEO of CapitalWize, Inc, quoted, "you can have everything you want in life, you just can't have it at the same time." This quote is so true and powerful when we think about all that we desire. It is possible to have all you want in this life, but there are seasons that you have to be patient and be willing to sacrifice pieces of your success in the moment so that you can nurture what you currently have in the present. Before walking through this journey of what you will gain, reflect on what you are willing to lose.

Producing Your Blueprint

In real estate development projects, blueprints give the crew a feel for what they are actually building so they can ensure the essentials are incorporated into the build while helping determine overall costs and project timelines. When we are producing the blueprint for our lives we must implore this same level of intentionality so we can understand what we are going after, what is required, the overall responsibilities and the average timelines that we would be able to achieve certain checkpoints along the journey. This helps us stay focused on our specific objectives and deliverables, while ensuring that we leave room for breaks and any contingencies that would lead to extending the project timeline. When you are producing your blueprint to navigate through your current season, it is important that you leverage the design, map and measure method below so that you can navigate around the storm before it even comes.

Design the Dream Out Loud With Purpose

I remember when I had my first custom home built and the process of being able to communicate exactly what I wanted, where I wanted it, and someone sitting on the other side of the table and simply taking notes and nodding their head. That person on the other side of the table as you begin to communicate your vision outloud is God and he is nodding his head, taking notes and using your actions, values, and commitments as the currency to see when he will give you a closing date on your dream. I read a quote by Pablo Picasso that stated, "every child is an artist. The problem is how to remain an artist once he grows up." The moment you stop dreaming is the time the clock that you are up against starts to speed up. I want you to stop reading at this moment and take out your phone and record yourself designing the dream out loud with a purpose. What do you want in your life? What do you want for your family? Talk to yourself about the type of experiences you want to create, the places you want to travel as well as the impact that you want to leave the world. As you are communicating, embrace the feeling that you feel and hold onto it. Send the vision video to the 10 people in your phone and ask for their support in helping you create the vision within a specific time frame. At the end of the video, challenge them to do the very same thing and send it to 10 people in their life as well. Imagine the impact you'd be able to have and the ripples you'd create just from sharing your vision with the world. It all starts with a record button, send and now the universe begins to work in your favor to create the very thing you envision. It's up to you to stop now and act now for the good of your vision.

Measuring The Cost Of The Project

The exciting part of the process is designing the vision out loud; the more stressful part comes in when we begin to measure the cost of the project. In life it's the same way when people say they want to be successful in business, marriage or successful as they approach their dream but aren't willing to commit to the responsibilities that come with wanting and achieving everything you envision. What you want is possible, but like in anything, if you don't have all of the capital up front to get everything you want, you build out everything over a period of time in stages. The question to ask yourself instead of giving up is what is absolutely necessary right now and what is the cost to get those very things? Once you understand that first step in the process, then map out your process and timeline and commit to the following steps in order to deliver on your commitment that you made to your vision. Oftentimes when we see the full cost of the project and we notice that we don't have it all, we give up entirely and have an idea that we will only come back once we have it all. Instead, I want you to change your mindset and invest portions over a period of time so that over time you can achieve everything you desire. Stop waiting to walk in your vision and begin to put the investments of time, energy, and resources towards your vision consistently so that you can be one step closer to closing your vision.

Drafting Your Squad

Relationships are a cornerstone of happiness and living a fulfilling life. They provide us with the comfort as well as the challenge that we need to feel supported while being pushed past our limits towards our success. When we are focusing on accomplishing new heights and reaching for new levels, it is important for us to draft a team of individuals that mirror where we are going, have shared visions and goals and are committed to the team winning. As you are creating the bank robbery of your dreams, who are the people that you need to pull off this purposeful heist? Here's a few people that you should draft to your team.

The Muscle - Rocked Wisdom

In every bank robbery there is always the person that has the physical "guns," or the hardware that is sometimes necessary for getting out of a sticky situation. In your life this person is the person that has the hardware of wisdom and serves as your counsel that keeps you grounded when your life seems to be getting out of whack. Usually this person would be older than you or maybe more experienced in the specific space that you need counsel in. They continue to guide you through challenges while having an unbiased opinion that's rooted in experience so that you can see all sides before making decisions.

The IT Expert - Systems Expert

You can not drive a car without an engine, and you won't be able to get through a bank robbery with a person that is handling all of the internal systems to ensure that you and your team aren't captured. On your team it's important to have someone that is process oriented and that thrives in creating systems and processes that navigate around challenges before they even come up. This person is the thinker and has the ability to solve problems on the fly that you bring to them. They don't just think in the moment, they are thinking 5-10 steps ahead and are willing to map out a plan so that you can code through life accordingly.

The Driver - Inspiration

Whether the person is driving a car or operating the getaway helicopter, who is the person that is leading you once you exit the bank to get you to your next destination. In life this person is the person that keeps you inspired, motivated and driven to keep going. They are either someone that inspires you, or continues to inspire you through affirmation, positive self talk or providing you resources that contribute to your wellbeing and happiness.

The Visionary - You

Remember, you are the visionary and the plan will only go as well as you planned it, through the obstacles as well as equipping your team around you. Your contribution is getting the people around you to be bought into the vision of what you are working towards as well as you being willing to receive support in accomplishing this tall task. What is your gift and skillset that will contribute to you pulling off the very thing you are working to accomplish. The visionary operates on their skills and strengths so that it allows the people around them to thrive so that a cohesive team is developed and empowered.

Tuning Up Your Engine

In a car the engine is a lot like the brain and it holds all the power necessary to help your car function. But what happens if there isn't an engine or if there is a repair that needs to be made that's causing the car not to start or function properly. Without the engine, the car would be nothing and without systems in your plan your car and vision won't move forward.

Minimize Clutter So You Can Maximize Speed

What is the clutter that is surrounding your life that you may need to remove in order for your car to function at top speed? Any relationships that are causing you unnecessary stress? Any commitments that you made that aren't in alignment with where you are going? Any habits or behaviors that you need to shift and eliminate so that you can be a bit more progressive? In a lot of cars today, if there is a problem with the car in any way it provides us a notification. Even if it is just a standard service appointment that needs to be scheduled at a certain point of mileage, the car notifies us.

Your body notifies you much more frequently than we give it credit and tells us through feeling overwhelmed, body feeling tense, or having a lack of clarity in certain areas. In the last chapter we talked about the importance of listening to our bodies and being willing to hear the answer and make the necessary adjustments. The same needs to happen as our cars are notifying us that we need to minimize some additional debrief that's causing our speeds to be slow or our car to not be at optimal performance. Assess everything around you and inside you and make the necessary adjustments by minimizing any clutter that isn't allowing you to move towards your purpose.

Performing a Systems Check

In a car's diagnostic system check it is a 14 step verification included that reveals problems with the car's engine, transmission, exhaust system, brakes and any other major component that may be affected. It's important for us to take ourselves through a system check of our mental, financial, personal, spiritual, relational, and emotional health as frequently as possible in order to check how all of these different areas are operating. When is the last time you've inconvenienced yourself, for yourself and took time to check in on your own wellbeing. We are so quick to check on friends, family and even our working colleagues, but we neglect to check on all

of our systems of our own vehicle. Follow the activity below
to check in on your systems.

Mental Health (1-10) What Do I Need to Do Better?

_____

_____

_____

Emotional Health (1-10) What Do I Need to Do Better?

_____

_____

_____

Financial Health (1-10) What Do I Need to Do Better?

_____

_____

_____

Spiritual Health (1-10) What Do I Need to Do Better?

_____

_____

_____

Relational Health (1-10) What Do I Need to Do Better?

_____

_____

_____

Personal Health (1-10) What Do I Need to Do Better?

_____

_____

_____

Professional Health (1-10) What Do I Need to Do Better?

_____

_____

_____

Keeping Your Goal in Front of You

How often do you see the goal that you are working to achieve? I could probably guess, not frequently enough. When we do vision boards, they end up under the beds. When we make goal oriented white boards, they end up being erased to create more space for other tasks or responsibilities. The first way to stay focused on the goal you are working to achieve is to see it every day as frequently as possible. Go into your phone calendar and two times a day, every day, set a calendar appointment with yourself to review your goal and the activities that you've committed to that day to ensure it gets accomplished. As goals get accomplished, you're able to form a habit of only focusing on specific activities that will help you achieve that goal. In this chapter we've laid out a roadmap for you to be able to start acquiring the very things you deserve and desire. It is up to you to continue to focus forward and use the activities that we've shared so that you can stay on track towards the vision you are working towards.

Feelings, Reflections and Actions

Use the pages below to write your feelings or reflections from the chapter or take this time to write out your action plan to begin YOUR BECOMING JOURNEY.

_____

_____

_____

_____

_____

_____

_____

_____

_____

_____

_____

_____

_____

_____

_____

_____

Chapter 4

WHAT IS POURED IN, FLOWS OUTWARD

"Your success will be determined by the quality of your relationships with people." - Danielle LaPorte

I f the only measure of your life were the relationships, conversations, and character that you exemplified, from a scale one to ten, how would the world measure you as a person? Would this same number confirm who the world sees you to be or have a negative impact on the perception that the world sees you as? I believe relationships are currency and hold a higher importance than money itself, but if we connect ourselves with the wrong relationships that don't align in values, character and integrity that this will leave our legacy bankrupt and our vision depleted. In this chapter we are going to help you identify the right individuals to help you accelerate your progress while guiding the parachute for you to land on the top of your mountop of manifestation.

Have you ever heard the phrase if you feed someone long enough, they will start to look like you? Well, that saying is true with who you get guidance and mentorship from, so be careful who feeds you and begin to look like them in action and in character. It's important to pray for what you want and use your discernment to ensure that what you are receiving is what God desires and not your lust for success. In this chapter you will receive an outline on how to assess relationships in a way that empowers where you are going.

The Five Most Important Questions

It is said that relationships are the breadcrumbs to our destiny, yet we don't take adequate time to assess, cultivate, and vet relationships in a way that helps us cultivate bonds that are beneficial to what we are building. As this chapter guides you to developing relationships that promote where you are going instead of exposing where you are, we want you to use these questions below to set the tone for what you need and desire from relationships moving forward.

- Does this person align with my core values and beliefs and commits to honoring my boundaries?

- Does this person challenge me to accomplishing my vision all while accepting who I am at the core?

- Does this person possess the resources, relationships or skillset to assist me with becoming the person I desire to be in the future?

- When I am around this person do I feel empowered, motivated, and inspired to be better each and every moment?

- Does this person's existence in my life make me feel peaceful, happy and joyful while helping me to achieve my goals and aspirations?

Relationships Are Future Reminders

The right relationships remind you of where you are going, not where you currently are or where you were. Have you ever had a friend that every time you get the chance to chat they continue to bring up stories that examine the past habits, choices, and decisions that you made and it seems as if they can't seem to move past, "the glory days," in their mind. If you are experiencing this or something similar to this, it is important to either run from that relationship or communicate a boundary that needs to be established in order to get the relationship on a track that feels more healthy and progressive. Relationships should be reminders of the future place that you are working towards, not consistent reminders of the seasons that have ended, the chapters that have closed or the levels that were already mastered.

When you think of who you desire to be, how does your current circle or tribe enhance the portrait? We often try to fit something into our lives; but what I've learned is that anything that is trying to fit, wasn't a priority in the first place and potentially is excess cargo that isn't necessary to add value to the specific relationship. Statistics show that good relationships help people live longer, deal with stress better, have healthier habits and have stronger resistance to colds.

Now these are all amazing statistics that continue to prove the importance of healthy and quality relationships and how they nurture and improve our overall lifespans. We must bring the same attention to toxic, unhealthy and damaging relationships and how they can increase stress, lead to decreased levels of productivity and happiness and cause potential heart issues.

Just as calendars hold us accountable to honoring our commitments, so do the right relationships in our lives. Relationships in many cases can be the accountability or reminder you need to get back on track and focused on the commitments you communicated prior.

As much as we can hold people accountable for their actions, words or commitments, I want you to be willing to receive the same level of coaching and be able to be humble as your friends, mentors, colleagues or team that you've drafted are working in conjunction to see you win. In the book The

5 Love Languages by Gary Chapman, the book explores the 5 different ways people express and receive love, calling them the love languages. The love languages of quality time, words of affirmation, gifts, acts of service and physical touch are the guiding principles of the book and the premise of the book explains that the faster someone discovers their love languages the sooner the relationship can be taken to new heights. I believe there is a sixth language that we can explore when we are dealing with purposeful relationships and the love language is progression and growth. It is important to adopt relationships that are progressive and promote growth and development in all aspects of life. I challenge you as you are reading through this chapter to assess and measure the relationships you have currently in your life and see if who you are next to can help you get into your next level and season.

Engineering The Right Environment

Whether you are building a car, a home, or your team that will help you create a life of fulfillment and impact, the engineering process is critical in the success of any of these areas.

At the core of everything, it is my belief that God should be the foundation to any environment that you are building. This serves as the measuring stick as you are assessing any future or current relationships and measuring them against the principals that your faith stands for.

Oftentimes our values and belief systems are rooted in our faith; so it is important for us to align with people that have similar values, beliefs and principles they live by. Whether you are building a relationship with a colleague, peer or a mentor, you don't want anyone in your environment that has a negative perspective, mentality or lacks the necessary character traits that align with who you are at the core. It's important to get around and stay around like minded individuals and build a community built on reciprocity.

Through this chapter we talked about the importance of building relationships that propel you forward towards where you are going rather than relationships that repel you away from your destiny. We provided you techniques as well as measurables to use that will help you assess the relationships that you currently have as well as the relationships that you desire to have in the future.

As you continue to read through the pages, master the steps that we've already covered before continuing to progress forward. We look forward to seeing you in the next chapter.

Feelings, Reflections and Actions

Use the pages below to write your feelings or reflections from the chapter or take this time to write out your action plan to begin YOUR BECOMING JOURNEY.

_____

_____

_____

_____

_____

_____

_____

_____

_____

_____

_____

_____

_____

_____

_____

_____

_____

_____

_____

_____

_____

_____

_____

_____

_____

_____

_____

_____

_____

_____

_____

_____

_____

Chapter 5

MISSION MANIFESTATION IS POSSIBLE

"The only way to make all of your dreams come true is to start believing in them." - Helen Barry

W hatever you want in life, you can produce as long as you learn how to weather the storm. Whether you see a storm as a disturbance in the atmosphere that brings rain or a storm as beneficial to washing away some of life's toxic attachments; storms are necessary in the progression of life itself. Storms produce the water that allow our plants to grow, which in turn helps us bear fruit to the world around us. Our storm signifies the challenges, experiences, and trials that we experience serving as the water that helps us become more resilient, conscious, and equipped to handle the responsibilities that come as we continue to progress forward.

So often, we pray for blessings and when we receive them we celebrate while committing to running away from the responsibilities that follow. We pray for rain, but if it rains too much, we complain. We pray for sunshine, but if it's too hot, we complain. We pray for happiness, but when it's too much, we question it by saying things like, "is this too much to be true," which in turn creates a space where we self sabotage the things we even want in our lives. How would you define your happiness and success and when you achieve it would you even be content and grateful for what you are currently experiencing? What I've come to realize is that the heaviest rain falls come from the storms that we least expect, didn't prepare for and weren't ready for potentially the result of its destruction. The first time I experienced a hurricane in life almost wiped me out and cost me everything I had.

It was one of those storms where you believed you were fully prepared, equipped and had all the necessary supplies. What was predicted to be a minor storm, with simple complications turned into an apocalyptic event that I was not ready, equipped or prepared for at all. I thought it was a time where I was bringing my team to a conference to advance themselves personally and professionally, but resulted in a cataclysmic event that ended up in the people abandoning me, leaving me feeling unappreciated, depressed, undervalued, and disrespected.

Was it because I was not expecting the result, or was I just not prepared for the storm? One thing I learned through this journey is that it is not about how you celebrate when you've received the blessing that you prayed for; the real test is how you fight during the storm that you weren't prepared for. The battle of the process that we are embarking on may make us feel unqualified, underprepared, and even unequipped, but in this chapter we are going to give you the steps on how to prepare, navigate, and make it through the storm stronger than when you walked into it.

Watching The Forecast

Wherever you are in your life now, it is important to continue to measure and listen to what your body is communicating on a consistent basis. Many of us look at the temperature daily before we choose what to wear so we can be fully clothed and prepared for what the weather is going to be like. We don't want to wear shorts if it is cold, wear a trench coat when it will be hot, or forget to pack an umbrella if it is going to be pouring down raining. In life it is important for us to watch the forecast consistently by leveraging the steps below so we can understand when the storm is coming, as well as be ready on how to navigate through its winds.

Measuring Your Momentum Thermometer (Sudden Drop in Temperature)

Research shows that a tell-tale sign of an approaching cold front is the drop in air pressure and temperature. In life a drop of mood, motivation, inspiration or changing in behaviors and habits is an indicator that something may be affecting your sunshine from showing up in your day. Have you checked in with your own internal thermometer and asked yourself, "How am I doing, really today?" If you are noticing a sudden change in motivation leaving you feeling sluggish, tired or even tense, I want you to take out a journal, reflect and provide an updated forecast on where your weather is heading.

If you continue this without stopping, taking a pause and reflecting on where you are, the storm will only pick up winds and get worse. Too many times through my journey, I neglected my own self because of this unhealthy codependency that I had to the image that I wanted people to see me as that I became so disconnected with what I actually felt so frequently. Every day, I want you to put on your calendar time to check in with you so that you know how many layers you need to wear during the course of the day. What you need matters, and the only way you can require and create boundaries around the things you need is by first understanding how you feel about yourself. Check in with yourself before your body checks out from you.

Minding Your Thoughts (Darkening Sky and Clouds)

When you see the skys darkening, you know that a storm is clearly approaching. As the clouds get darker, it signifies that there is a lot of rain in them and a part of a thunderstorm. As your clouds get dark in your life, it isn't healthy to keep your thoughts and feelings in a cloud, it is important for you to release anything out of you that can't contribute to where you want to go or who you want to become. What are some thoughts that you have about yourself or the things that you are involved with that don't bring clouds that are clear, but rather bring clouds that are filled with self limiting and defeating thoughts and perspectives?

What are the things that you need to rethink or ways that you can reset how your view of the world is skewed? In science, the severity of a storm is related to cloud height, which is why dark clouds are usually an indicator of bad weather. In life, the longer you hold on to what isn't helping you inside, you will ultimately not only hurt yourself but the things around you that hold meaning. As you feel your clouds darkening, use meditation and positive brain exercises to make yourself a personal priority for you. It's important to focus on your long-term vision of what you want and imagine the impossible being accomplished. Over time as you learn to navigate through your stormy emotions, it will allow you to face whatever is thrown at you.

Checking in On Your Behavior Patterns (Changes in Wind Direction)

What have your behaviors and actions been saying about what you think about yourself and the others around you? What have you done that can contribute to your growth or consequently contribute to your unhappiness? We must have intention with all the areas where we perform so that we can ensure that we are remaining powerful and precise in our purpose fulfillment. Check in on what you've been doing so it can begin to tell a more detailed picture on what needs to be done moving forward. When we think about what our behaviors are saying about ourselves and where we are going in life, it will allow us to course correct, re-route and get our boat back on track. Ask yourself these three questions:

1. Are my behaviors over the last 2-3 weeks progressing

me forward or keeping me where I am?

2. How have my behaviors been making me feel lately?

3. Are these behaviors attached to some feeling that I am not working through resolving?

Preparing Your Land For Heavy Winds

In Isaiah 54:17 it states, "no weapon formed against you shall prosper, and every tongue which rises against you in judgment you shall condemn. This is the heritage of the servants of the LORD, And their righteousness is from me,"Says the Lord. During this verse God is speaking to us and telling us that the enemy will try to work against us, but it will not work if we continue to trust in our faith and position ourselves next to him.

In all of your different seasons, it is important to prepare for other heavy winds and storms by positioning yourself closer to God. Here are three steps below that will help you take action immediately prior to the storm arriving at your doorstep.

Getting Your Home Essentials

What are essential things in your life that make you feel happy, free, and fulfilled? Whether that is a specific journal that you love writing in, a book that you just can't stop reading, or a relationship that brings you life and allows you to open up your perspective? As you are preparing yourself and getting yourself ready to navigate life's storm, it is important to attach yourself with things that are essential and serve as an important part of your peace.

As you are reflecting on what these items may be, I want you to consider three things. You want to have something to help you reflect, recharge and feel refreshed.Use these few questions below to help guide you through this period.

1. When I need time to reflect, what do I do, where do I go and with whom do I feel most at peace?

2. What helps me gain my energy back after I feel depleted? What helps me get back on track?

3. What excites, inspires or motivates me to keep going?

Once you answer these three questions above, identify the best course of action to implement these back in your life or in your life on a more consistent basis.

Fueling Up For The Storm

During a thunderstorm may be the worst time to pump gas so it is important to get all of your food and gas before the storm hits. It is my belief that the best way to energize and fuel up is to take time to control your stress, lighten your load and get adequate rest. Too many times we are in work mode that we don't recognize how much could actually be accomplished if we were fully charged.

In the last section we challenged you to ask yourself three questions that you can reflect, recharge and feel refreshed. As you prepare to fuel up for the storm here are a few questions to reflect on.

1. What can I implement into my daily schedule to show that my physical, emotional and mental health are a priority?

2. Is this my season of pushing the gas pedal or maybe

putting the car in park? What have I felt towards either of these options?

3. Am I taking enough time to actually take time and allow my body and mind to rest?

Boarding Up The Windows

The last measure to take as you prepare for the storm, is to board up the windows or set boundaries that will not allow anything to get you off track. In the book, Balance by Toure Roberts, he states that, "balance is not about time management it is about boundary management." It is important for us to better manage our time, attitude and experiences by best managing the boundaries that we set in our lives that will allow us to get everything that we desire.

What measures do you have to put in place in order for you to protect your purpose and create barriers around what you are building? Here are a few questions to reflect on as you are working through creating the boundaries.

1. What are boundaries that need to be put in place with people in my life that would help me better

focus on my specific priorities or actions?

2. What are boundaries that I am neglecting to set because I fear judgment or discomfort?

3. What is one boundary that I need to make now that would help me become more productive or fulfilled immediately?

The Sun Still Shines Behind The Clouds

Whether or not your dreams seem cloudy your sunlight will continue to shine in the midst of clouds. In many cases, when we experience turmoil, challenges or even barriers in the pursuit to building our dream, we stop seeing the light at the end of the tunnel. Joshua Marine quotes, "challenges are what make life interesting. Overcoming them is what makes life meaningful." Challenges are a part of the great mystery of life and are necessary throughout the journey of self actualization and discovery. As you experience challenges or feel your clouds overshadow your vision, here are two things to consider every time.

Identifying The Root

Whether in business or in your own life, performing a root cause analysis is a useful process for understanding and solving a problem. By understanding what negative events are occurring or peeling back the curtain behind the effects of your experience; it allows us to alter our trajectory at a root level and not solve the symptoms. Too many times we are not actually solving the problems, because we are putting bandaids on symptoms. When we are able to look at the complex systems around problems, identity triggers and key points of failure, hold ourselves accountable as well as being responsible for the new direction, that is how we are able to create change within our lives. When you initially realize a challenge that you are experiencing, it is important to first ask yourself, "What went or what is going wrong?" Once you are able to reflect on what is going on and how it is making you feel, start to think through the patterns of actions, behaviors or decisions that you made that put you in this specific position.

I believe that the patterns of our behaviors can tell us how far we really are away from our purpose if we just pay attention. With every behavior or action, there is a set of consequences that follow that you will be able to draw a conclusion from. Once the conclusion is reached, now it is time for you to implement the necessary changes that will promote growth and success moving forward. Ask yourself these questions below.

1. What do you see happening and how is it making you feel?

2. What are the patterns of my behavior that are causing me to feel this way?

3. What is the recurring theme that I continue to run into?

4. What is the next best step that I need to make moving forward that is different from what I am usually used to doing?

Searching For The "Who"

Once you've understood the root cause of the problems that you are working to solve, it is important that you begin to recruit the people that can help you accelerate the learning curve that are experts in areas where you are experiencing challenges. Who is a person that has mastered what you are trying to learn? Sometimes we have to look outside of our current network in order to get connected with the person that can connect us with our calling. Before you just start searching for the person you need, I want you to become the person that person would want to engage with. The best relationships are reciprocal and are mutually beneficial, so ask yourself, "What can I learn, where can I grow, or what can I provide the person that can help accelerate my growth?"

Growth is a process and a journey not a sprint, so if you want it badly enough, you're going to have to be able to withstand the pain and discomfort that comes up along the way. Anything that has grown tall, was initially planted and experienced a season of darkness. But through the process of nurturing the seed, providing times of sunlight as well as pouring the necessary water to help the seed's growth process, the seed over time provides the shade for the next genera-tion. Before you are able to elevate in your life, you must go through a season of pruning that feels like pain, but it is helping you gain the stamina to have the power you need once you reach your purpose. I challenge you to find your who, by first searching within yourself and asking, "who do I need to become, in order for the people I need to welcome my value?" You are valuable, you are deserving and you are worthy of all the things you desire in life, now it's up to you to begin working on those things to become the person that you were called to be.

Feelings, Reflections and Actions

Use the pages below to write your feelings or reflections from the chapter or take this time to write out your action plan to begin YOUR BECOMING JOURNEY.

_____

_____

_____

_____

_____

_____

_____

_____

_____

_____

_____

_____

_____

_____

Chapter 6

PERMISSION GRANTED

"Life is a book. We write in everyday existence." - Lailah Gifty Akita

I heard a story once about a mom that was trying to teach her daughter confidence. It was a Saturday morning and the mom needed a specific ingredient to cook breakfast, so she sent the daughter to the grocery store across the street to get this key ingredient to make the meal. She got back home and the door was locked. After 10 minutes of knocking on the door aggressively to over power the music that was inside, she picked up the phone and called her mom to have been met with anger and frustration because the mom realized that she gave the keys to her daughter prior to her leaving the house. The phone hung up and the daughter realized that keys were in her hand as she held the phone the whole time. A lot of times we are calling on friends, colleagues or even neighbors for the solutions to our challenges not realizing that God has already given us the keys to our calling that we have been holding on to the whole time.

We're calling around to man, instead of trusting our faith to open the doors that we have been in front of through so many seasons. In this chapter it is time for you to give yourself permission to change, transform, and elevate to the heights that you envisioned as we began our conversation in chapter one. We walk around life standing in front of the doors of opportunity not realizing that the keys are in our hands the whole time. We want you to pick up the keys of your purpose and unlock the doors of power so that you can enhance, empower and equip the world with all that you've been called to innovate.

Rest, Revise, Release

True freedom is about being yourself without the world's permission. Whether you are wanting permission for the relationship that you are currently in, the business that you are wanting to build or the school that you are wanting to attend; the quickest way to experiencing peace and a sense of freedom is by not allowing the opinions of man to be the determining factor of if you are permitted to where God has already called you to be. There are three areas that are important to consider as you are working to break the chains of "their" opinion so that you can begin to follow "His," plan.

Resting is the new hard work

Rest in this generation is the new hard work because it is so important for driving productivity, bettering mental health, increasing concentration and memory and improving the overall mood and your metabolism. Napoleon Bonaparte quotes, "The best cure for the body is a quiet mind." Too often we associate rest with lack of productivity, laziness or stagnation, but rest in fact is the complete opposite. It is important to allow your body the time and freedom to rest so that it can be able to recharge as you work to tackle life's hurdles. In a world full of stressors, responsibilities and activity, calming the mind and body can be challenging, but it is essential to physical and mental restoration.

The human body isn't built to last marathons that last forever, it is built to thrive in a series of short sprints and bursts as we focus on completing life's marathon. Taking a break, even for only a few moments or ours allows you to refresh, recharge and replenish anything that has been lost so that you can preserve your way through the rest of your day. As you continue through your journey, implement in your calendar times for rest and relaxation just as you implement times for productivity prone activities.

Consistently revise your decisions, choices and habits

There's a saying in entrepreneurship that, "Yesterday's price isn't today's price." The phrase connects to the importance of a customer understanding that as the value increases the prices may reflect an increase as well. The same is true when we are thinking of our decisions, choices and habits. Motivational Speaker and Youth Pastor, Chris

Thomas, quotes, "When everything changes, everything must change." This is so true within our lives and we must understand that when you feel, experience and desire a change, the decisions, choices and habits that once felt normal and comfortable must also shift and change as well. Who you desire to be is dependent on how you respond to conflict, the choices you make under pressure and the habits that you form as you are growing through your process. Consistently revise your decisions, choices and habits to reflect where you are going and not always reflect where you currently are.

Release habits, relationships, and anything that is no longer serving you

The only way that you are able to heal and grow is by releasing and not suppressing. You have to get comfortable with surrendering to your feelings and emotions, and now suppressing your feelings and emotions to appease a relationship that no longer serves you. Too many times in our lives we don't want to offend the people in our lives but it results in us offending our purpose because those relationships aren't allowing us to progress or be fully who we are destined to be.

In the book of Psalms, David writes in Chapter 139 verses thirteen and fourteen, "for it was You who created my inward parts; you knit me together in my mother's womb. I will praise You because I have been fearfully and wonderfully made."

Don't ever forget who you are and why you were put on this earth. If there is a relationship or anything that is no longer serving your season, it can no longer be a part of your story. Use the steps from previous chapters to set boundaries, identify your peace, so that you don't ultimately create patterns of behaviors that lead to your unhappiness and unfulfillment.

Don't Let YES Bankrupt You

In my career I've had the privilege of attending conferences, sitting in boardrooms, and being in rooms with some of the most elite people, to only recognize these are the same people that are so poor, that the only thing they have is money and wealth. The secret to success is only found in how well the desires of your heart align with what you know is true in your soul. When your actions and desires align, that is how you know you are operating on purpose. This requires discernment, boundaries and building able to honor yourself through forgiving yourself.

Learn how to say no so that the yes to yourself is empowering

The power of saying no in a world of access to "yes," will help you accelerate your growth and ultimately protect your peace. When we say, "no," we are valuing ourselves in a way that promotes mental and emotional health and it starts by first setting boundaries that honor what you need and where you desire to go in life. Valuing your time is a brave act that takes courage and is the best tool to create distance and space away from negative people, situations or events that may not promote who you desire to be in the future.

When is the last time you've inconvenienced yourself for yourself in a way that felt comfortable, joyful and fulfilling? Every time we say yes, it takes away from the capacity to use that same time, resource and energy towards the yes that progress towards our purpose. Before your next, "yes," measure the cost of what in fact is actually costing you. Before we can maximize our life, it must take simplifying and minimizing the things that don't promote where we want to go. Where are areas that we can minimize in order to profit from our deep desires? Can we minimize contact with certain people, spending in certain areas, or time given to certain entertainment? Sometimes it isn't about completely stopping and replacing, because that wouldn't be realistic, it is about minimizing the time and resources that we put in specific areas so we can maximize our creativity, innovation and space to promote another area.

Creating Your Own Mantra

A few years ago, I had the opportunity of being in professional development training and at the end, the speaker had us end with a "Mantra" to say out loud together as a group. She believed that as we are walking into reimagining our new direction in customer experience, it was important for us to make a declaration out loud together that would create an energy in the room filled with togetherness, community and teamwork. Since that moment, I've believed in mantra's, their power and what they can do to create the results that we need whether in our personal or professional lives.

It is said that a mantra is a sacred prayer that can be repeated out loud or silently to instill peace and tranquility throughout all times in your life. Whether it is an affirmation, declaration, or commitment, it is important to allow your mantra to be the landing strip that you go to every time that you feel you need to make an emergency landing. What you want, believe you will become and feel as if you must have started with the belief in your mind and follow with the declaration of your words. Follow the prompt below to write your mantra statement.

I am _____ (describe who you are and who you desire to be)

_____

_____

_____

I will _____ (describe the actions that you will commit to, to create that type of life)

_____

_____

_____

I have _____ (describe the things you have that you are grateful for or the gifts that you possess that can help you become the person you desire)

_____

_____

_____

I am ready to _____ (describe what you are ready to see happen in your life and why it's meaningful to you)

_____

_____

_____

I believe _____ (describe your beliefs about yourself, the world and how it will all work together to support your vision for your life)

_____

_____

_____

Now I must _____ (describe your immediate actions and decisions that you must take to have growth)

_____

_____

_____

Embracing Your Significance

At the end of your time here on earth, what matters is
not our success that we have acquired, but our significance
that we've created through the contributions of our calling.
We must understand that success will help us achieve awards,
accolades and temporary recognition, but to achieve significance is to achieve the highest honor and that is for our names
to never be forgotten.

Moving From What If to What Is

Do you often find yourself consumed with all of the factors
of what possibly could happen as you are progressing towards
your future success? Rather than thinking about all of the
possibilities of what could potentially happen? If this is anything like you or resonates, then you're stuck in the factor of
what if, rather than what is. What is is that you are strong,
you are worthy, you are deserving, you have all of the skills,
resources and information that you need to progress forward.
But if we continue to be stuck in the what if, and consume

ourselves with negative self-talk with all of the self limiting beliefs or problems, they will end up consuming our progress and take away the power that is needed to get to our purpose. I read a quote once that said if we focus on problems, it's going to end up creating more problems.

But if we focus on the possibilities that exist, then it will end up creating opportunities that we didn't even imagine could happen. If you can see it in your mind, you can hold it in your hand. All it takes is belief and throughout all of the chapters of this book. We have helped you understand the importance of faith, belief, what you're envisioning, so that you can have a clear roadmap and picture on what is possible in your life. It is time for you to move away from the negative what ifs and start moving forward to all of the what is of your life by focusing on the possibilities, the opportunities and the greatness that is already in store. One activity that I would implore you to focus on through this process is every time you think about a potential problem that comes up, I want you to cross it out and write a solution right next to it. In every in every setting. When we think about problems, ask yourself what is the best next step that needs to take place that can get me through this current circumstance and closer to my calling.

Stop letting the doubt distract you from developing what God has already decided for you

Having faith just isn't about believing when things are going in the way that you want them to go. It's about remaining consistent, committed and believing through the challenges, the storms and all of the hurdles that will come up through the process of reaching our purpose. We must stop letting doubt distract us from developing what God has already decided for us. We must stay focused on our vision in hand. And everything that we envision throughout this whole book throughout all of the chapters must be at the top of our mind, inserted into our spirit and be the guiding roadmap that through any challenge through any roadblock or any hurdle that potentially comes up, that we're continuing to believe in anything that you're doing in life. There's going to be challenges that come up. There's going to be times that you don't necessarily believe in the outcome.

But as long as we are committing to the process, and falling in love with the challenges and asking ourselves new questions and inquiring more about ourselves throughout these processes so that we can ask ourselves, who do I need to become to get through this rather than what do I need to do to get through this, then we will be successful. If you can become the person that is necessary to get through that challenge. Then you will be able to hurdle through all of life's challenges that come through you. I implore you to ask yourself that question. Every time you meet a new challenge, who must I become to overcome this rather than what I must do?

Your story is significant because what you've gone through is someone's roadmap right now

Everything that you have been through is significant. The challenges that you've experienced, the pain that you have felt, and the moments where you wanted to give up are all significant. And the reason why is because you have made it to this point where you're able to work through the pages, not only of this book, but of your life in a way that shows that you are an overcomer you are a redeemer, and you are strong enough to progress and persevere through life's many challenges. There are so many people in life that need your story, who need to hear what you've experienced and how you've experienced some of the toughest times in your life that have helped you become the most beautiful person that people get to experience now. Your story is significant because what you have gone through is someone else's roadmap right now on how they get through it.

So it is important as you are continuing through this book as we move into the conclusion that you share your experiences that you've gained, all of the knowledge that you have learned, as well as all of the techniques that you have implemented within your life as you have read through these pages that have helped you but also can help others on their own journey. We are excited to work with you and partner together to debunk all of the lies of becoming the person that you are destined to become and the story we hope that you've recognized your power that you've understood your calling. And you've received the necessary resources and techniques so that you can become the person that you were destined to become. As we move forward into the conclusion, I challenge you to ask yourself this one question. If you don't reach your purpose, who is negatively impacted? By not focusing, remembering who you are and choosing despite any circumstance to follow your calling.

Feelings, Reflections and Actions

Use the pages below to write your feelings or reflections from the chapter or take this time to write out your action plan to begin YOUR BECOMING JOURNEY.

_____

_____

_____

_____

_____

_____

_____

_____

_____

_____

_____

_____

_____

_____

_____

_____

_____

_____

_____

_____

_____

_____

_____

_____

_____

_____

_____

_____

_____

_____

_____

_____

_____

_____

_____

Chapter 7

BIRTHING THE CEO WITHIN

"To become a leader, then, you must become yourself, become the master of your own life." - Warren Bennis

One of the biggest misconceptions that people have about me is that I am not a mom, mom. What I mean by this is the mom that cooks, cleans, takes care of the family and husband, while still maintaining the strength, resiliency and power to build a seven figure brand that is expanding across the world. And one thing about me as a mom, is that I absolutely love to cook and I recognize with any amazing meal, there are certain key ingredients that are necessary to ensuring that the meal comes out in the way that you envisioned it in your mind with macaroni and cheese, per se, without the eggs it won't stay together in the oven. And sometimes we are so quick to throw our dream in the oven without going through the necessary checklist of key ingredients that are critical to the meal's success.

This chapter is about you slowing down in trusting in your faith throughout the process, while understanding God has always given you grace and mercy, as long as you remain faithful, action oriented and obedient as a part of the process. Having the perfect strategy is not necessary. But belief, faith and action are the necessary ingredients for success as you stand in your power on purpose as we move through our concluding chapter. One of the biggest things that I want you to understand is how to mix up your masterpiece. ferment your future and prove your purpose so that you can bake your dream with belief.

Mixing Your Masterpiece

What are the ingredients that are necessary for you to pro-duce the type of bread or success that you desire? In creating bread? The basic ingredients are flour, yeast, water and salt. In life, the basic four ingredients are faith, action, environment and mentality. When we talk about faith being our foundation, that is the rock, not the sand that is that everything is built on within our life. If we don't have the necessary belief to see our dreams before we're actually able to hold our dreams, through the storms and hurdles and obstacles that we're going to encounter throughout the journey. It's going to be challenging for us to continue to prevail in the face of pain.

Faith is Your Foundation

As you set faith as your foundation, I want you to get clear in your vision and what you really want. I want you to get so clear that you can actually feel, hear, see and taste the actual vision that you want and who you need to be now so that you can become that person in the future is absolutely necessary, with faith being your foundation and a belief in something bigger than yourself. Whether that is trying to create something for the community around you or stop generational curses from being able to happen or just building a faith based relationship with your family that's built on character values, principles and integrity. Whatever is really important to you is important to keep the foundation in front of you and leverage that as a mission and vision declaration so that it can continue to be the guiding principles for your whole life.

Empower Your Environment

When we begin to understand that faith is our foundation this will allow us to empower our environments around us because if our relationships in what we have around us is not in alignment with the beliefs, principles and the values that our faith represents. Then it's going to be challenging as we've talked about throughout this whole book, to be able to create an environment of success if we're not planting the right seeds and producing the right fruit around us. If we have a bunch of weeds around us, then it's going to end up affecting or potentially blending in with the fruit that we have in the same garden. So before you even plant anything in your life or any people in your life, it's important that you clear the land in leverage faith as your foundation, and you specifically and intentionally put the right seeds in the ground so that all of them can grow together and in turn be able to grow you when you're able to have the right people around you it's it gives you the ability to be able to accelerate your work ethic accelerate your productivity, as well as being able to put you in a position of continuous inspiration, accountability and motivation.

Increase The Ceiling of Your Mind

When we begin to understand how and feel the effects positively from our environment, empowering us. This will give us a sense of mental stability, clarity, and empowerment in our mind. That is important for us to be able to go to the next steps within our lives as we begin to increase the ceiling of our mind and what is even possible within our lives. This will allow us to look at different perspectives as opportunities and not just as problems as we talked about throughout this whole book. This will allow us to meet people and discern if this is the right relationship. That should be a part of our story. As we're moving forward. We'll be able to set quality and firm boundaries within our life that will protect our eyes by being able to enforce our nose. This will increase the level of opportunities that we create as well. I tell students all the time that when I speak to them, you are a product of your three to four best friends that you spend most of your time with. If you think through and take an audit of your conversations, actions, activities that you do with your specific friendships or colleagues or peers that you spend most of your time with. What does that really say about your current circumstance? A lot of times we were so critical of the people around us and saying that they're not helping us or not providing us with what we need to be successful. But we continue to still find comfort in those spaces because we don't have the courage of stepping up for ourselves and stepping out and away from those situations so that we are able to have the very things that we need to be able to progress and move forward until you're able to step up for yourself. And step away from those spaces. You will have a decreased sense of exposure to what actually is possible and you'll only see the world from a skewed perspective. If you really want to be able to increase the ceiling of your mind and the ceiling of what is possible. You have to involve yourself around people that are actually doing things now that you envision to do in the future. And once you're able to effectively understand how to put faith as your foundation. Empower your environment, increase the ceiling of your mind then you'll be equipped and prepared to take deliberate action. When we're taking deliberate action. It's up to us to be able to focus on our priorities, not just activities that need to be achieved. A lot of us get into this mindset of this long laundry list of tasks

that should be shrunk. As we magnify God within our lives, and the more that we magnify Him, the more that all of the different things that we see as important that we see as problems are minimized throughout our journey as you're progressing through the rest of your life, as well as through the rest of this book.

Take Deliberate Action

It's important for you to take actions that directly align with your priorities and priorities that directly align with your purpose. If we're only taking purposeful, intentional, deliberate action, then we're setting up ourselves for success every single time. So as you're navigating through the waves and through the journey of your life, it is important for you to ask yourself consistently, does this action or do these sets of decisions or choices directly benefit where I am trying to go? If it does not benefit directly where I'm trying to go? Then you need to have the courage, the discipline, as well as the foresight to say no to those things now before it potentially becomes a problem later.

Fermenting Your Future

After the dough is mixed, it is left in a warm place in the kitchen to ferment until it doubles its volume. During this process the yeast cells start to consume sugar and release carbon dioxide gas which helps a rate the dough at the same time producing assets and alcohol. During the time of fermentation, what you consume and release will ultimately require you to produce boundaries, heightened expectation, and an unwavering commitment to what it is that you're trying to accomplish in the first place. I am not a master baker, but I am a master manifester. And it is possible that these same characteristics may be seen as acidic and flammable. So those around you but that truly shows that they aren't meant to join you in the process of your development.

Building Boundaries That Benefit You

When we focus on building boundaries that actually benefit us, adding a hint of exposure, understanding how to commit and allow that commitment process to be our concrete. There's no way that we're not going to be able to set ourselves up for a successful future as we look at building our boundaries that benefit us. A lot of times we've had a negative relationship when it comes to boundaries. We think that this means that we're not supposed to talk to our friends, we're not supposed to go out or we're not supposed to do anything that actually brings us some type of joy, or fulfillment and are specific lives or even a sense of happiness. When you're building boundaries that benefit you. You're really just asking yourself, what are the things that I need to do in this current season? What is helping me progress towards my purpose? And what are the things that I need to maybe minimize, potentially cut off for a period of time, or just stop doing all together that have been historically seen to remove me or pull me away from my very purpose that I'm actually trying to focus on? When you're building boundaries that benefit you you're only focusing on for periods of times and spurts and short sprints on the things that can push you forward towards where you want to be, rather than entertaining and giving time, resources and energy to the things that are keeping you where you are. It is more challenging to say no, than to continue to stand like me in so many different areas within my life that I've talked about in previous chapters to be that people pleaser and say yes to all of the opportunities, all the parties and all the financial ways that you can grow your specific life as well. What boundary do I need to set right now? That gets me to where I need to be tomorrow is a question that I continue to ask myself and a question that I would implore you to ask yourself as well.

Add a Hint of Exposure

When you begin to set boundaries, it allows you like we talked about in the last section to increase the ceiling of your mind. And now you're able to add a hint of exposure so that you can begin to see different things that you weren't able to see because you were so distracted in that period of time. Whether you're spending a week by yourself going on a writing vacation, or taking time away from social media, clubs, or even secular music. I would ask you and want you to sacrifice something for a short period of time so that you can receive the clarity that you need that will last you a lifetime. What do you notice in your life that you're spending time doing that isn't really benefiting you in the way that you would want it to benefit you, but you continue to do it to fill time or waste time, but that time needs to be magnified or maximized in other areas. What I would recommend that you do within this reflection period is to remove that for a series of hours, days or even weeks. And start reflecting on the things that you gain and the experiences that you create and the knowledge that you learn and all of the information that can help you push towards your purpose and not pull you away towards stagnation.

Commitment is Your Concrete

Once you commit to the process of exposing yourself through setting quality boundaries that benefit you. Now commitment needs to be concrete. There are going to be so many times where you do not want to do something as a part of you growing in your season towards becoming successful. But commitment isn't about going to the gym. Budgeting or telling the truth when it benefits you and that moment or when you want to do it. Commitment is about creating a system that benefits you for the long term and remaining committed to that system even though you don't feel like it at the moment. When we understand and we commit to the goals within our lives. There's a financial goal, a personal goal. Or a professional goal that we're trying to achieve. We have to honor our word to ourselves before we can expect the world to honor their word to us and commit to all of the things that you say. And before you actually commit to it, reflect on the responsibilities that come prior to your commitment. A lot of times we're making commitments but we're not reflecting truly on the responsibilities that come. So I would implore you to ask yourself what is this going to take to do this and am I actually ready within this season to do it? And if it is a yes it is up to you to use commitment as your concrete so that you can see the process through.

Proofing Your Purpose

Proofing is the next step in the process and it is when the dough begins to rise in the tin, container or dish you are preparing it in. In baking, the dough will double its size before you bake roughly in about 2 hours, and in life if you're pouring the right ingredients inside your recipe, you will also double in size of mind, vision and perspective in the time that you remain committed to the process. It's important in this step to implore some form of temperature check on yourself to ensure that you are ready for baking.

Temperature checks are necessary to ensure you are fully equipped and prepared to leap before making mistakes that cost you everything that you've worked for. There is a thin line between being perfect and being prepared and only you know where the line rests. I want you to think through how you want to feel, how you currently feel and how far off you are from being able to experience the very thing you want that can help you produce the type of success you want to experience. Don't let perfection paralyze your ability to perform well, but also don't perform ignorantly without knowing what you are up against. Remember that baking and preparation is a process, so don't just before the recipe and the oven is at the right temperature.

Baking With Belief

Preparation without production is simply a waste of time, energy and ingredients. This is where many people don't make the final step that is the most important. And that is why baking is the most critical step in the bread making process. The time and temperature are similar to the pressures that will arise once you step into your calling, and start to wear the crown that God has placed on your head. Two things that we want you to understand before you close the pages of this book are to set a celebration timer and to stop measuring the picture against the progress.

Setting a Celebration Timer

When we are focused on setting a celebration time or what this means is declaring a date that you would want this recipe to be finished. Oftentimes we have arbitrary goals. That we never set clear measurable bowls for and that is why we don't reach them, or we don't feel the pressure or holding ourselves accountable for what is required to actually accomplish that goal. With any recipe, there is a specific time that it shouldn't be in the oven. If you leave it in the oven longer than the time that it may overcook. If you take it out before the time then it may undercook. So what you want to be able to do and make a habit of is put dates specifically to what you want to accomplish within your life.

And if you miss the day, then now you review what are the reasons why. But if you accomplish it before the day, that really just shows in life that you are over delivering or setting goals that are too easy, and that needs to be a bit more challenging. It's a challenging process. However, I want you to get into the habit of putting dates to everything that you're trying to accomplish and align the responsibilities, actions choices, and hold yourself accountable to be able to stick to those specific dates. When we think about the pictures that we see on the internet. That leads us to wanting to make that recipe, get the ingredients and cook that meal for our families.

Stop Measuring The Picture Against The Progress

Oftentimes the first time we cook something it does not end up in the same way that the picture shows it. This often leads us to disappointment, discouragement, and it doesn't really have a connection and maybe how the taste of it is but we focus so much on the picture and not the progress or the completion of what we've been able to accomplish in your success journey. I don't want you to be focused on the pictures of what success looks like. I want you to be able to focus on the taste and what it feels like once you accomplish it. Too many times we're comparing our story and our journey of success with other people's journeys and I don't want you to get so caught up in that.

That is one of the lies of becoming and throughout this book we have talked about how important it is to set the foundation of your faith. We've talked about the importance of understanding how you set boundaries. We've wanted you to become a better us so that you can be able to build a scalable business and I've told you about my challenges that I've even experienced as a woman, as a mother and as a wife, so that you can be able to design the life that you envision. There's a clear difference between good ideas and the ones that God has in store for you. But it's just up to you to be able to manifest those things. And understand that what is being poured into you in your relationships and the knowledge and what you're exposed to is what you are pouring out into the world. So if you want to flow closer to your purpose is calling and get out of that circumstance. It's important for you to understand that you are granted permission not by man, but by a higher power.

I am so excited and thankful that you've shared this journey with me and we've been able to have this amazing conversation. I hope you've at least left with one or two things that you have either already implemented or that you can implement moving forward that will be able to shake up and shift your journey and even how you view yourself. If there is more information please if there are more questions, please follow the pages to find out how to get in contact with our team and we're so excited to serve you moving forward. Good luck and we love you.

Feelings, Reflections and Actions

Use the pages below to write your feelings or reflections from the chapter or take this time to write out your action plan to begin YOUR BECOMING JOURNEY.

_____

_____

_____

_____

_____

_____

_____

_____

_____

_____

_____

_____

_____

_____

_____

About Author

Meet Tanya Sanders-Kelker

Tanya Sanders-Kelker is the founder and Chief Executive Officer of Profit and Growth, a small business consulting and accounting firm committed to helping business owners create systems and strategic plans to increase profits and scale their companies. In 2017, Kelker combined her entrepreneurial gift with her experience as a beauty professional and founded Body Party Wax and Beauty Studios, growing an automated system that produced an additional six-figure income, positioning her as a thought leader in the beauty and services industry. As a two-time graduate of Jackson State University and a member of Alpha Kappa Alpha Sorority, Inc., she is committed to serving her clients to create the business of their dreams with order, strategy and purpose.

Proud wife and mother of three children, Tanya currently lives in Jackson, Mississippi. To find more information about Tanya Sanders-Kelker email her at admin@tanyaskelker.com.